Poetry about a girl.
Just a girl,
Living her life.
Writing down her dreams.
Just a girl.
Imperfect and flawed.
Found her love,
Inside of herself.
Writing some words.
Words that became poetry.

Empower Herself

shell.chelle

These words became a story.
Her Story.
A story of a girl who:

Lost Herself

Found Herself

Then learned to...

Love Herself

In order to. .

Empower Herself

This little side note:

This is her experience.
Her point of view.
Her feelings.
Her perspective.
Her story of letting go.
Her story of leaving,
A world of black and white.
Leaving the darkness,
And finding her light.
Her story of arriving,
To where the grey area resides.
This place of surrender.
This place of light.
A story of her memory.
A story of her truth.
A story from her eyes.
A story from her heart.
A story from her mind.
A story that she remembers,
As she listened to herself.
As she listened on her path.
Her path to self-love.
Her path to self-worth.
Her path to authenticity.
Her path to alignment.
Her path to her soul.
Her path.
Her love.
This is her story.

Also, this.
(In very fine print.)

These words.
These are just words.
Words of poetry.
Poetry to read.
These are just words.
Beautiful words.
Words of poetry.

Empower Herself

Empower Herself

She wants to change her expectations.
Her expectations into preferences.
She wants to change her demands.
Her demands into choices.
She will no longer rely.
Rely on them emotionally.
She will no longer over-give.
She will no longer people-please.
She will no longer be someone she's not.
She is not responsible for their problems.
They are not hers to carry.
She will become who she is meant to be.
She will follow her heart.
She will rely on herself.
She will be there for her emotions.
She will stop searching.
Searching for it all outside of herself,
Looking for love.
Looking for support.
She didn't believe.
Believe in herself.
She needed to find,
Trust in herself.
She needed to figure herself out.
She needed to understand.
Understand herself.
She needed to give compassion.
Compassion to herself.
She needed to love.
Love herself.

Love herself,
Before she could empower herself.
She needed to meet.
Meet this little girl.
This little girl inside of her.
Her inner child,
She needed to meet.
Meet her and nurture her.
Hold her and love her.
She needed to heal this little girl.
She needed to figure out what she needed.
Listen for her needs.
Listen for her voice.
Listen and tune in.
This is her time.
Her time to find her worth.
She is holding it now.
Holding her worth.
With care,
She holds it.
Holding her worth.
She knows her worth.
She understands herself,
She understands her preferences.
She understands her standards.
She understands her choices.
Her choices she makes.
It is up to her.
Up to her now.
She will stop putting her worth,
In everyone else's hands.
She knows her worth.

It is her turn now.
It is her turn now to hold her own worth.
Holding her worth,
In her own hands.
Holding her worth.
Holding her love,
As she empowers herself.

The Strongest Girl I Ever Knew

I will accept that I came from a world.
A world I didn't belong in.
A world I never fit into.
I will accept that I didn't belong there.
I will accept that I need to grieve.
I need to grieve where I once was.
I need to grieve that life that I lived.
I need to grieve myself...
The girl I will leave behind.
Because the only way to go,
Where I want to go...
Is to leave that beautiful girl.
I need to leave her behind.
She helped me so much.
She took care of me.
She protected me,
When I needed it.
She was the one there for me.
She was my rock.
She was the one.
She was the one,
Who called the shots.
She made the decisions.
She took the risks.
She showed no emotion,
While doing all of this.
She was the strong girl,
The girl who never gave up.
She was the fighter.
She was numb.

I can't be her...
Not anymore.
I need to leave her behind,
To go where I have to go.
This is so hard.
This grief that I have.
This grieving for the girl...
That girl that I was.
I cry these tears.
These tears are for her.
Looking back,
To see all that she's done.
Living in survival mode,
Just so she can breathe.
Wearing her mask,
Just to be accepted.
Staying in this illusion...
Inside of that façade.
Just to be part of something,
Just to be loved.
The fixer.
The doer.
The pleaser.
The fighter.
The lifter.
The girl with a smile.
The girl who was always good,
All while shoving everything down.
Walking around numb,
As she got everything done.
Pretending everything was fine,
Because she didn't know how to stop.

She didn't know how to cry,
She didn't know how to rest.
She didn't feel safe,
She would run away.
She didn't know how to communicate...
She didn't take care of herself.
She took care of everyone else,
While shoving herself aside.
The strongest girl I ever knew,
Is this girl I need to say goodbye to.
I don't need to be her anymore,
Because I walked away from everything.
Everything I knew.
A whole world,
That I never fit into.
This was *her* world,
The world she knew.
This world was hers,
She knew just what to do.
She knew how to live.
She knew how to survive.
She knew how to be...
She could be numb here.
She could be in survival mode here.
She could show no emotion here.
She could be good all the time here.
She could have a smile on her face,
When she just wants to cry.
She could have no voice here.
She could be dismissed here.
She could have walls up around her heart here.
She would be manipulated and controlled here.

She would be surrounded with expectations here.
She would know conditional love here.
She would be the strong girl here.
This world was made,
For masks and façades.
Illusions and walls.
Walls around her heart.
This world was made,
For black and white.
This world did not know,
Shades of grey.
This world did not accept her,
As she changed.
I need to leave this beautiful girl...
I need to leave her here.
Here,
In this world.
This world was her comfort.
This world was her safe space.
I am showing her a new world,
As we leave that old world.
And as I do this,
I need to grieve her.
Grieving the strongest girl I ever knew.

Empowerment

Oh,
This empowerment.
I am empowered.
Take my power back.
Take it back now.
Those low vibrations,
Shrug them off.
Oh,
This empowerment.
I am empowered.
I am empowered by using my voice.
I am empowered each time I speak.
Each time I speak.
Each time I listen.
Listen to myself.
Listen to my soul.
Listen for my intuition.
It tells it all.
I am empowered.
This empowerment that I found.
I want to be inspired by the people around me.
Oh,
You don't stay the same.
Oh,
You don't tell me what I want to hear.
Oh,
You speak your truth.
Oh,
You speak your mind.
Just speak it all.

Anything you want to say.
I value your words.
I value you.
If that's what you need to tell me,
Then I will hear you.
I will honor you and hear you,
If that is what you need.
I value the people,
Who just say it how it is.
Just speak your mind,
Just speak your truth.
I want to feel inspired,
By the people around me.
The people around me,
You all inspire me.
Thank you for your inspiration.
Your inspiration helps me to grow.
Your inspiration brings empowerment.
I am empowered.
Empowered now.

Higher and Higher

Find those people.
The people who bring you higher.
Higher and higher.
The people who let you evolve.
They evolve with you.
Level up.
We are all going into higher vibrations.
Be with the people,
Who empower your growth.
Empower your soul.
Higher and higher,
We are all lifted up.
You are lifted,
So am I.
We are evolving.
Evolution is higher.
Higher and higher.
We keep going higher.
Growing and releasing.
We do not go back.
We move to new places.
We do not look back.
We release the old.
We release our baggage.
We no longer carry with us,
The weight we once carried.
Find those people,
Who let you evolve.
Evolve and grow,
Level up and change.

Find those people…
The people moving higher.
Higher and higher,
We are lifted.
We are all lifting.
Lifting our vibration.
Evolution is here.
Come with me.
Come with me,
Or stay.
Stay back there.
I must go,
Higher and higher.
Are you coming?
Coming with me.
Evolve and grow,
Higher and higher.
I will not stay the same,
I will not go back.
I will never go back,
To where I once was.
Higher and higher,
Stay on track.
Release what's old,
Get rid of it now.
Higher and higher,
The only direction I'll go.

Understand My Soul

Now I understand.
I understand my soul.
My soul was never connected.
Connected to my wounds.
My soul has been covered.
Covered by pain.
Covered in black.
Covered by darkness.
My soul has been my light.
My light all this time.
My light has led me.
Led me to love.
My light has been leading me.
Leading me to my heart.
My heart has been bleeding,
But not anymore.
My heart was in pieces,
But I picked them all up.
I picked them up,
And held them.
I held them and loved them.
I acknowledged each piece.
I broke down these walls.
As the walls came down,
I found my soul.
My soul had no illusion.
The illusion was gone.
My soul was clear.
Clear to me.
I felt connected.

Connected to my soul.
My soul is light.
My soul is love.
My soul will lead me.
Lead the way.

Your Heart Knows

Your heart has rejected,
What is not right for you.
Your heart has rejected,
What is not in alignment with you.
Your heart will tell you.
Your heart knows.
Your heart will lead you...
To where you have to go.
Your heart has rejected,
What is not for you.
It always told you,
It has never let you down.
You just needed to find trust in yourself.
Trust in your heart.
Because your heart knows.
You lost trust for a little while.
You were not connected.
You lost the connection.
You found the connection.
You found the trust.
Trust in your heart,
Like never before.
Your heart has led you,
To where you are now.
Your heart is here,
To tell your soul.
Your heart knows.
It can feel what's right.
Trust in your heart.
Trust in what's right.

Trust in surrender.
Surrender and let go.
Let go of it all.
That's what you have to do.
Your heart will tell you.
Appreciate this.
Your heart will guide you...
All the way to surrender.

Shove It Under The Rug

Shove it away.
Shove it under the rug.
Hurry.
Quick.
Don't look at it.
Don't look into it.
Just shove it under the rug.
Put it away,
For another day.
Another day,
That will never come.
Because subconsciously,
You want to avoid everything.
Another day after that other day.
Another day passes.
Hurry,
Just keep putting it away.
Get your broom.
Sweep it away.
Keep sweeping until you see nothing.
Until you feel nothing.
Hurry,
Get the broom.
Sweep it away.
Once again.
Keep on sweeping.
Sweep it all away.
Just get it away.
Put it away.
Shove it down.

Push it all down,
Until you explode.
Until it all comes bleeding out.
Bleeding out onto others.
Bleeding out onto others,
Who do not deserve it.
Hurry get the broom.
Get it out again.
This will work this time.
I'll just sweep more this time.
Once again,
It bleeds...
It comes pouring out.
Exploding out.
It is explosive.
Just put the broom down.
Throw it away.
This method doesn't work.
Can't you see that it doesn't even work?
Deal with it as it comes...
You won't need the broom.
This way is smoother.
Your stuff won't pile up.
Deal with it as it comes.
This will take strength.
This will take patience.
Patience with yourself.
Give yourself grace,
As you pick up the pieces.
Putting the broom down...
This takes empowerment.
This takes time.

Time that you think you don't have,
Which is why you have this broom.
But are these explosive episodes worth it,
When it ruins each relationship, you have?
Are these inappropriate reactions worth it,
When you bleed onto the ones you love?
I put my broom away,
Never again will I live that way.
This method does not work.
It simply just does not work.
All of those piles that you shove away...
If they aren't bleeding out onto others,
They are manifesting in pain.
Put that broom away,
Sort through your piles.
Every single pile,
Is waiting for you.
Waiting for you inside.

Some People

Some people you just connect with.
Some people you can just read.
Some people you can just see.
You just see their aura.
You just see who they are.
You see who they are,
Just by observing.
Some people you can just feel.
Feel without any touch.
Some people you just hear.
Hear them without having them speak.
Some people you just get.
You just get them,
You understand.
Some people you just know,
Without having to go deep.
Some people you just have a soul connection with.
This soul connection makes you feel close.
Some people are just by your side,
Without ever having to ask.
Some people just give,
Because they see what you need.
Some people just call.
They just call to say hi.
Some people just support you,
And you hardly even talk.
They let you live your life,
And expect nothing in return.
Some people just smile.
They just give you a smile.

They just want to make your day better.
Just because that is them.
Some people are just there.
Out of nowhere they appear.
Some people run to you.
Run when you are not well.
Some people just send love,
Just to let you know they care.
Some people are just so genuine.
That is all they are inside.
Some people are just filled with so much love,
And they just want to give you some.
Some people just want you around,
They just want you to sit.
Sit and enjoy.
Sit and relax.
Some people just want what's best for you,
And that is all that matters to them.
These kinds of people,
Have changed my life.
These kinds of people,
I am so thankful for.
These kinds of people,
Thank you for existing.
Thank you for existing,
In what sometimes can be a cruel world.
Thank you for not getting sucked away.
Sucked away by ill intentions.
Thank you for not getting pulled into...
Pulled into this bitter world.
Thank you for not closing your heart.
Closing your heart each time you get burned.

Thank you for surviving your grief.
Surviving your losses and your traumas,
You have been through so much.
Thank you for keeping your heart open,
After all of that pain and hurt.
Thank you for working on yourself enough,
So that you won't ever lose yourself.
Lose yourself to cruel intentions,
And a harsh world.
Thank you for seeing me clearly.
Thank you for loving me.
Thank you for hearing me,
And understanding me.
You all are beautiful.
Beautiful to me.

Be Still

Stillness will tell you everything.
Everything you need to know.
Be still.
Do you hear?
Do you hear the sound of your own voice?
Do you hear this?
Do you hear these answers?
These answers you are being given,
Straight from your intuition.
All it took was stillness.
Silence and solitude.
Do you hear?
The sound of right now.
Do you hear the sounds of this moment?
Do you see?
Are you seeing your dreams?
Are you seeing your reality?
Are you seeing this clarity?
Be still.
Do you understand?
Understand what is within you.
Can you feel?
Can you feel these sensations.
These sensations in your body?
Be still.
Can you hear the beating of your heart?
Can you see the horizon out in front of you?
Can you feel the warmth of the sun?
Can you appreciate this very moment?
Do you have appreciation,

For this stillness?
For this silence and serenity.
Be still.
Can you feel this clarity?
Can you feel this aura?
This aura around you?
This aura of love and light.
This love and light is you.

The Other Side Of The Illusion

This illusion I had,
I had it to feel safe.
This lens I looked through.
This lens of denial.
Because I didn't want to see the truth.
This illusion I had,
Was to cover the bad.
I couldn't handle what was really going on.
I didn't want to see.
I didn't want to admit.
I didn't want to feel.
Feel uncomfortable emotions.
This illusion kept me small.
Kept me there for everyone else.
This illusion kept me from myself.
This illusion kept me running.
Running in survival mode.
Running from the truth.
This illusion kept me from standing up for myself.
This illusion kept me from having a voice.
A voice that was mine.
This illusion controlled me.
Controlled who I was.
I couldn't see reality.
Because my lens was fogged.
I couldn't see myself.
Because I was living with this illusion.
It wasn't until I questioned this.
Questioned this illusion.
Questioned reality.

Questioned the truth I knew.
Questioned my denial.
It wasn't until I challenged.
Challenged everything I knew.
Asking myself questions.
Questions I had never asked.
Questions that were scary.
Questions that rocked my world.
Questions that I didn't really want answered.
Questions that didn't make sense.
Challenge what you know.
Challenge your world.
Challenge yourself.
Challenge your inner world.
Challenge this lens you look through.
Challenge your illusion.
I asked myself why.
Why, a million times.
I asked myself questions.
Questions that started this journey.
Very simple questions.
Questions that brought me here.
Questions that brought me to my freedom.
Freedom is on the other side.
On the other side of this illusion.
This is where I found my freedom.

Cycle Breakers

Those cycle breakers, though.
The people who break the cycle.
The people who change the world.
The people who speak up,
When their voice does not want to be heard.
They still speak anyways.
They say what they have to say.
Their voice matters.
Because of all the times it was shutdown.
Their voice matters.
Because of all the times their voice was crushed.
Those cycle breakers,
Bring the change.
Unwanted change.
Unasked for change.
Those cycle breakers, though.
The people who see.
They really see.
They see what is really going on.
They know the truth.
The people who speak.
Speak the honest truth.
The people who have fear,
But they still go on anyways.
The people who question society.
The people who question beliefs.
The people who don't follow guidelines...
Because what are guidelines anyways?
The people who can't be controlled.
They can't be kept on a leash.

The people who question the surface,
Because what is underneath?
The people who do it differently.
Differently than the rest of the world.
The people who make their own little world,
Instead of doing as they are told.
The people who walk into a room,
And they don't care if they are liked.
The people who have a purpose.
The people who call you out.
The people who say it how it is,
Without having any fear.
The people who still send love.
Send love to the people who burned them.
The people who still have forgiveness in their hearts.
The people who speak the truth,
But they do it with love.
Those people who are so genuine...
So completely genuine.
Those people who just love.
Those people who make time for you,
When you need them the most.
These are the people,
Who change the world.
These are the people,
Who change you.

This Smear Campaign

The name calling.
The belittling.
This smear campaign.
These things you say.
Say about me…
Keep them coming…
This says more about you,
Than it does me.
And the people who believe it…
It's okay.
I know who I am.
And you don't even take the time to get to know me.
You have no clue who I really am.
Because you spend more time away from me.
Believing rumors,
That are not true about me.
You spend more time gossiping about me.
Assuming you know me.
Than actually sitting down,
To hear my side of the story.
It's okay.
You can believe what you want.
It's okay.
You can assume what you want.
I am done putting any effort in,
To make people see.
I am done trying to fix a problem,
That keeps showing up repeatedly.
The same exact problem,
That is concocted secretly.

This problem that was made intentionally.
This problem that is not mine.
I am done having the knives thrown at me.
I am done nurturing the wounds,
Left from these knives.
These knives,
Being thrown by the person creating the problem.
That no one wants to see,
Because they are all looking at me.
Blaming me,
As I have the knives thrown in my back.
Stuck in my back.
These knives,
Were thrown by the person you don't want to see.
All because,
You are too busy looking at me.
It's okay…
I will be over here.
Living my life blissfully.
Living my life…
Finding genuine people.
Who do take the time to get to know me.
I will be over here,
Walking away from people like you.
Walking away from people living in an illusion.
Walking away from façades and masks.
Walking away from gossip.
Walking away,
From name calling and smear campaigns.
I no longer have room,
To be someone I'm not.
I no longer have room,

To make myself small.
I no longer have room,
To be put down.
I no longer have room,
To be punished and controlled.
I have lost all trust in people like you.
I no longer have room,
For your judgement and opinions.
Judge me.
Belittle me.
Gossip about me.
Talk about me.
I no longer make room,
To worry about this.
These are your problems,
Not mine.
The next time you speak my name...
Ask yourself questions.
Why is this concerning you?
Why is,
What I am doing affecting you?
Are you proud of the words coming out of your mouth?
My name coming out of your mouth,
Has more to do with you...
Than it does me.
I will be over here,
Living blissfully.

I Can Change My Mind

At any given time,
I can change my mind.
Nothing is permanent,
Everything is temporary.
I can change my mind,
At any given time.
There is no permanence.
Nothing is permanent.
It is all temporary.
It comes,
And it goes.
This flow of life.
This flow of feelings.
None of it is here.
Here to stay.
It is here,
To be acknowledged.
Acknowledged,
That is it.
Then it is gone.
This flow.
This state.
It comes and it goes.
It is here,
Then it is gone.
It comes,
And then it leaves.
Flowing through life.
Life is a flow.
Nothing is permanent.

My mind can change.
It can change,
At any given time.
Feelings are fleeting,
I can change my mind.
Everything changes,
This is a constant.
Nothing stays the same,
This is the truth.
Nothing is permanent,
Everything is fleeting.
Let everything come,
Let everything go.
Enjoy this moment.
This moment,
As it is.
This moment is fleeting.
Enjoy it right now.
This moment is new,
I can change my mind.
I can change my mind,
At any given time.

Walk Your Walk

When you walk the walk.
Walk this walk.
Walk your walk.
This walk is for you.
The path you pave.
This path is hard.
This path is for you.
And no one else.
This walk.
Your walk.
It is for you.
Layers in the way.
These are barricades.
Barricades that are standing in your way.
Barricades that have been placed.
Strategically,
For your journey.
Barricades for you,
To pick up and work through.
They are not to climb over.
They are not to be shoved to the side.
They are specifically there,
For you to pick up.
Pick up and go through.
Go through this pain.
This barricade,
This layer that has been in your way.
This layer of pain,
That has been holding you back.
Once you move through it...

Cry those tears.
You will be lighter,
On the other side.
The other side of this barricade.
These barricades are placed along the way.
When you walk your walk,
You choose the path that is not paved.
You have chosen the path,
With barricades and pain.
It is not the easy way.
This walk that you walk,
Will be worth it in the end.
This walk that you walk,
Is freedom in the end.
You just can't see it,
While you are walking your walk.
Listening to your gut,
Following your heart.
Let these words comfort you along your walk...
These barricades are the keys.
The keys to your love.
Each barricade you pick up,
Holds a key.
A key to your worth.
A key to your love.
Your own self-love.
A key to your trust.
A key to your intuition,
As you follow your gut.
These keys you collect,
Will bring you comfort on this path.
As you walk your walk.

This walk is for you.
This walk is not easy.
You have chosen the hard way.
The path that is not paved.
It is up to you to pave it,
Along the way.
You have no idea what you are doing.
You have no idea how to do this.
But you keep on going.
Walking your walk.
You do not give up.
This path is rocky.
This path is unknown.
This path has no direction.
You just keep collecting your keys.
These keys are your crown.
Your crown that you wear.
This crown you create.
You create with these keys.
This crown you will wear.
You will wear at the end.
At the end of this walk.
This crown,
That you wear.
You will wear this for,
The rest of your walk.
You are the queen.
The queen of yourself.
The queen of this walk.
This walk that you walk.

Speak Your Truth

Do you want to find your people?
Just speak your truth.
Live your life.
Say what you really want to say.
Say what you feel.
Speak your truth.
Tell the truth.
No hesitation.
Just say what is real.
Be direct.
Be honest.
Be ready for backlash.
Be ready for the reaction.
Be ready for anything,
With no expectation.
Your people.
Your crew.
Your tribe.
They will stand by your side.
They will allow you to speak your truth.
Say what is real.
They will support you,
On your journey.
Of using your voice,
No matter what.
They will support you.
Love you.
Hear you.
See you.
Understand you.

There they will be.
Your true people,
Don't leave you.
They make that appearance,
When times get tough.
They say those words,
That lift you up.
They let you be.
They allow you to live.
Live however you choose to live.
Speak your truth.
Say what is real.
You are not here to be walked on.
You are not here to be abused.
You are not here to be ignored.
You are not here,
For everyone else.
You are here,
To live your life.
And whoever comes along,
For the ride.
This is how you know,
You have found your tribe.

Your Temple

Your body is your temple.
Nurture it.
Believe in it.
Love it.
Your body is your happy place.
Breathe into it.
Your body is your temple.
It will be with you always.
It is the thing that will never leave you.
Your body will be with you.
With you,
For life.
With you,
Until the end.
The end,
Of your time.
So, treat it with care.
Nurture it.
Listen to it.
What does it need?
Your body is your everything.
It will love you unconditionally.
Unconditional love.
Breathe in.
Breathe out.
Your body is yours.
All yours.
It is your temple.
It holds your soul.
Your soul's protector.

Your soul's protection.
Your body,
Your protection.
Connect with your body.
It holds every answer.
Every answer,
You are trying to find.
These answers are not found,
On the outside.
Those answers are within you.
They are inside.
Deep inside of you.
Past the layers.
Each layer you pick up.
Each layer you hold.
Each layer you acknowledge.
Brings you closer to your soul.
Your body is your temple.
This beautiful temple of yours.
Love it.
Care for it.
Nurture it.
Love it.
This is your temple.

She Was Born To Be Free

She was born to be free.
She was just born to be free.
From the very beginning,
She was just born to be free.
No one just let her be.
Allowed her to be.
Allowed her to go,
Where she needed to go.
Allowed her to be a free spirit.
Because that is who she is.
Who she is at heart.
A spirit born to be free.
She was born to be free.
She was not born,
To follow the rules.
She was not meant,
To follow a script.
She was not made,
To be controlled.
On her own.
This is her.
This is her soul.
From the very beginning,
She was born to be free.
She was just born to be free,
In her own little world.
Wild and free.
Peace and serenity.
This is who she is.
The core of who she is.

Soft hearted and genuine.
Gentle and loving.
Forgiving and easygoing.
This is who she is.
She was born to be free.
She was just born to be free.

My Crown

This is my crown.
Do you love it?!
I legit gave my life for it.
I let go of it all,
Just to wear this crown.
Do you like my crown?
This cost me my all.
Everything I knew.
Everything is gone.
Do you like my crown?
Is this crown worth it?
Worth my tears.
Worth my pain.
Worth it all,
Going away?
Do you like my crown?
A lesson I learned,
Along the way.
A lesson I learned…
This is my crown,
And many won't love it.
But that is okay,
If you don't approve.
I have learned not to be liked.
Not everyone will support me,
And that is okay.
If you don't approve…
I have learned that not everyone will like me.
Not everyone will support me,
And that is okay.

Not everyone will like my crown.
Not everyone will support me wearing this crown.
Not everyone will help me with my crown.
I have learned to love myself.
And in order to find,
This love for myself.
This might mean...
Disappointing others,
And leaving some behind.
This might mean,
Not being liked.
Not being loved,
By the people around me.
Not being loved,
By people in my life.
That is okay.
Because for so many years,
All that mattered to me,
Were other people's crowns.
Let me help them put on their crown.
Let me help them become a Queen.
Let me help everyone else,
By tossing myself aside.
Sacrificing my own crown.
Sacrificing my own love,
To love everyone else.
Holding up everyone else's crown.
Their crown to put on.
Their crown to wear.
"Where is my crown?
I will look later...
Her crown matters more than mine."

Giving all of my love away.
Setting my crown aside,
Every single time.
Because that is who I am.
Unconditional love.
Completely selfless.
Too selfless,
At times.
When is it my turn?
My turn is now.
I found my crown,
And it is time to wear it.
It is time for me now.
This crown I will wear.
It is finally time.
Time for my crown.
It is finally my time,
To become the Queen that I am.
I am my very own Queen.
I left a whole world behind,
To wear this crown.
This crown, that is mine.
This crown,
I hold up.
I hold this up for me.
Naming myself Queen.
Queen of my world.
My own little world.
I wear this crown now.
My own little crown.

This Peace That I Found

This peace that I have found.
This quiet.
Serenity.
This peace that I found.
After I left the chaos.
This peace that I found.
I will not give this up,
This peace that I found.
It came with a price.
It cost me my all.
All that I knew.
My whole world.
A world that I knew.
A world that I left.
This world that I left,
So that I could find peace.
Peace.
Quiet.
Calm and serenity.
This peace that I found,
I won't let this go.
This peace that I found.
This is all I ever wanted.
I won't let this go.
This peace that I found,
Is where I found love.
Love for myself.
This pathway of peace.
The early part of this path,
Was completely chaotic.

Noisy.
Frantic.
Go.
Go.
Go.
Autopilot on.
Living in survival mode.
Filled with challenges,
Hardships and pain.
Chaos and confusion.
Goodbyes,
So many goodbyes.
Followed by grief.
Nurturing my nervous system,
Finding peace.
Breathe in.
Breathe out.
Finding my breath.
Connecting with my body.
Connecting with my heart.
Finding my soul.
This peace that I have found.
This path has not been easy.
This path was not always peaceful.
This path tore me up.
Tore me up,
Inside.
This path wore me down,
But I got back up.
I always get back up.
This peace that I found now.
Let me just be here.

Let me just sit here.
Let me just feel this.
This is amazing.
This peace that I found.

Subtracting

She's had enough people subtracting.
Subtracting from her life.
She's had enough people taking.
Taking her love away.
She's had enough people,
Using her.
Using her to meet their needs.
She's had enough people,
Controlling her.
She's had enough people,
Stomping on her heart.
Trampling over her,
Like she is just the ground.
The ground that they walk on.
She's had enough people,
Betray her.
She's had enough people,
Leave her.
She can't do it anymore.
Letting go is what she does.
Letting go is familiar.
Familiar to her.
Letting go is what she knows.
Letting go is her comfort zone.
Letting go has become her norm.
All this letting go.
She will take this peace.
This peace and solitude.
Herself, is who she saved.
She saved her a million times.

She saved her from the people.
The people subtracting from her life.
She saved herself from chaos.
That chaos is all she knew.
She thought this was life.
This chaos that she saw.
This chaos that she lived.
She thought this chaos was love.
That chaos was subtracting.
Subtracting from her own self-love.
She never knew herself.
Herself filled up with her own love.
She is getting to know her now.
She found her inner peace,
As she sorted through her demons.
She found this peace.
This peace in her heart.
She found this peace.
This peace is her new start.
This peace is here to stay.
This solace.
This quiet place.

Our Interactions

Our interactions.
They are so easy.
Our interactions.
They don't take any work.
Our interactions.
We pick up right where we left off.
Our interactions.
We pick up like no time has passed.
Our interactions.
Are just so comfortable.
Our interactions.
Feel like home.
Our interactions.
They are just so easy.
This is the energy.
Our energy.
The energy between us.
It is so organic.
The energy between us.
It just feels so right.
The energy between us.
It is a happy place.
This energy between us.
Is give and take.
I never feel drained.
Drained by you.
I feel filled up.
You are filled up too.
I feel the love.
This love that you give.

I feel your light.
This light that you are.
Our interactions.
They are just what I need.
Our interactions.
They are beautiful to me.
Our interactions.
Our connection.
Thank you for being you.

Just Sit

Please just let her sit here.
Sit here in this peace.
Sit here in this quiet.
Sit here in this solace.
Sit here in this bliss.
There is no noise.
No chaos.
There is nothing to hear.
There is nothing to do.
Rest.
Just rest.
Just enjoy this peace.
Listen to this quiet.
There is nothing to hear.
No words to be said.
She is burnt out.
Burnt out from a life.
A life that she lived.
A life that she left.
She is burnt out.
She just needs to be.
Let her just be.
Let her just sit.
Sit in this peace.
Sit in this grief.
These waves will pass.
But for now,
These waves are here.
Peace for her.
She found this for herself.

No plans.
No commitments.
No expectations.
Just peace.
Just quiet.
Just living her life.
Living her life of peace.

Nothing Is Left

Following what is in alignment.
Alignment with my soul.
Following what is in alignment.
Alignment with me.
Following my heart.
Trusting in myself.
Surrender it all,
Until there is nothing left.
Nothing but love.
Attachment is gone.
Grounding myself,
To connect to my soul.
Clear it all out.
There is nothing left.
Losing it all.
Detached from it all.
Listening to my soul.
Following that voice.
This voice gets louder,
As I clear it all away.
Let it all go,
So, I can follow this voice.
Let it all go.
There is nothing left.
Let it all go.
It is so clear.
The fog is gone.
I can see clear.
Let it all go.
Get rid of it all.

There is no more noise.
Nothing to hear.
Silence is left.
Clear it all away.
Follow my heart.
Detach.
Nothing is left.
Nothing but love.
Nothing is left.
I am free.

She Is Burnt Out

She is burnt out,
From transactional love.
She is burnt out,
From all of the work.
All of the work,
That she had to do.
All of the work,
That she had to put in.
Becoming a person.
A person she wasn't.
Just to be loved.
Just to be accepted.
Just to fit in.
She is burnt out,
From transactional love.
Let her just be.
Just be here now.
She is burnt out,
From the manipulation.
She is burnt out,
From all the expectations.
These expectations put on her.
She is burnt out from being dismissed.
She is burnt out from being shut down.
She is burnt out.
Burnt out from it all.
She is just burnt out.
She needs to rest.
Doing it all,
On her own.

Supporting herself.
Making every decision.
Every decision,
Is up to her.
She is burnt out.
She needs to rest.
Everything is gone.
Let her grieve.

This Beautiful Whisper

She lived with fear.
She lived with this fear.
Her whole life,
She lived with this fear.
Fearing the people.
The people in her life.
Fearing that love,
Would be taken away.
Love that she needed,
Because she didn't love herself.
She relied on everyone else.
Everyone around her,
Gave transactional love.
Love with expectations.
Love with conditions.
If I do this for you,
You do this for me.
I expect you to do this.
I expect you to say this.
I expect this and that.
I expect you to be a certain way.
I expect so much,
Out of you.
I expect you to perform,
And be your best.
I expect you to be happy,
At all times.
I expect you to be who I want you to be.
I expect these transactions.
These transactions from you.

And if you do not act,
How we expect you to act…
We will leave you.
Punish you.
Dismiss you.
Ignore you.
Whatever we decide to do…
This transactional love.
You must be this way.
You must keep your mouth shut.
You must not fight back.
You must do it our way.
Talk the way we expect you to talk.
Answer our questions the way we expect.
You must do for us,
Whenever we call.
Be there for our emotions.
Be there to listen.
Be there when we are down.
Whatever we expect.
You must not get tired.
You must not rest.
You must not change.
You must not grow.
We will not give you any space…
It is about us,
And our needs.
And if you do try to communicate your needs,
And it is not something we want to hear…
We will leave.
God forbid,
You speak your needs.

God forbid,
You even speak up.
God forbid,
You stand up for yourself.
God forbid,
You stop accepting our shit.
God forbid,
You become your own person.
God forbid,
You deal with your own emotions.
You are supposed to be there for our emotions,
When we are down.
You are supposed to do as we say,
Because we are in control.
This is how she lived,
For a very long time.
This is how she lived,
Pushing herself aside.
This is how she lived,
Until she decided.
Until she decided,
She was worth more.
Until she decided,
She would love herself.
Until she decided,
Her worth is in her hands.
Until she decided,
Her love is in her hands.
Until she decided,
To meet her own needs.
She has needs too,
And they will no longer be ignored.

She saw this beauty.
This beauty in her.
She started seeing her gifts,
Her gifts in her.
She started finding her talents,
That she had never known before.
She started connecting with her creativity,
And her intuition.
She started to listen.
Listen to the voice.
This voice that was shoved down.
Shoved so deeply down.
She started to listen to,
What started as a whisper.
This whisper she heard.
This was HER.
And she listened.
She listened,
Finally.
This whisper,
Became louder.
This whisper,
Became clear.
This beautiful whisper.
This beautiful voice.

Honor Her Voice

To honor myself,
Is to honor my voice.
Honor what I have to say.
Honor and respect.
Respect myself.
Respect my truth.
I am who I am.
I will speak my truth.
I will not be walked on,
Not anymore.
I will not be taken advantage of,
Not anymore.
I will honor my voice,
By speaking my truth.
I will say what I have to say.
I will not hide.
I will do what I want.
I am free.
I found my peace.
I found my voice.
I found my worth.
I am worthy.
I will not hide.
I will not be brought down.
Brought down to the ground.
Just to be walked on.
Walked on and used.
Walked on and scolded.
Walked on and abused.
Those days are over.

Those days are done.
I walked away.
I walked away for good,
Never looking back.
Those are the days.
The days I didn't believe.
I didn't believe in myself,
At all.
Those are the days,
Where I lived for everyone else.
Everyone but me.
Everyone but myself.
Those are the days.
Those days in the past.
Those days, I grieved.
I put them away.
I am not that girl.
That girl is gone.
That girl who was walked on.
Walked on and stepped on.
Walked on and used.
That girl with no voice.
That girl is gone.
That girl will forever,
Honor her voice.

This Beautiful Peace

Make life beautiful,
From the ugliness.
Take the ugliness,
And turn it into beauty.
Always into beauty.
That ugliness.
That pain.
It will be turned around.
Turned into beauty.
No matter what.
Take the terrible,
And turn it into gorgeous.
Turn it into something pretty.
That beauty came from ugliness.
That beauty came from pain.
That beauty came from something awful.
Take the chaos,
And turn it into peace.
Use your breath.
Breathe in.
Breathe out.
You are at peace again.
Take the madness,
And turn it into brilliance.
Magnificence and light.
These miracles came from turmoil.
This turmoil was turned around.
Turned into excellence.
Excellence and love.
Turn the storms,

Into sun.
Turn the rain,
Into clouds.
Turn the turbulence of thunder,
Into the calm sounds of the birds.
Turn these hurricanes around.
These hurricanes will pass.
These hurricanes soften.
Soften into a breeze.
This soft breeze is here now.
You can finally breathe.
Your breath is your peace.
Your peace and solitude.
You are at peace.
This peace that you found.
You took the ugliness,
And you turned it around.
You turned it into beauty.
This beautiful peace.

Always Running

Always running,
Running from herself.
Always running,
To receive any kind of love.
Always running,
Towards everyone else.
Always running,
To please everyone else.
Always running,
To be there for them.
Always running,
Running from herself.
Always running,
Towards transactional love.
This was familiar.
Familiar to her.
Love me with conditions.
Always running,
To meet their every need.
Always running,
To fill their cup.
Always running,
Running from herself.
Running from her own love.
Running from her soul.
Running from what was inside.
Inside of her.
Running from her pain,
While running from her heart.
Running from her worth,

Because she didn't believe in herself.
Surrounded by people,
Who couldn't see her.
Surrounded by people,
Who didn't let her be.
Surrounded by people,
Who wouldn't let her speak.
Let her speak her truth.
Let her speak what was real.
Oh, and if she did...
They would leave.
She wasn't understood.
She was kept on a leash.
This leash of control.
Kept in this cage.
This cage of transactional love.
Kept there with manipulation.
She was punished if she tried to leave.
Obey their rules,
Or else.
"You must be there for us."
She would cater to every reaction.
She was blamed for being herself.
She was scolded if she needed distance.
She was held responsible for their feelings.
She really did love them unconditionally.
But this was too much work.
Too much work,
While she needed rest.
She just needed rest.
She needed to find herself.
She needed to fill her cup.

She needed to repair her heart.
She just needed some space.
Space to be herself.
She needed out.
Out of this cage.
This cage filled with conditions.
This cage filled with expectations.
This cage was so black and white,
And she just wanted to see the grey.
She kicked that door open,
And off she went.
She kicked open that door,
She was free.

A Walk, Through Codependency

Walking through codependency...
It is not about them.
It is about you.
Stop worrying about them.
Worry about you.
They are not your problem.
Stop giving unsolicited advice.
Stop walking on eggshells.
Just say what you feel.
Just be real.
Be authentic.
Have your boundaries.
The way they react,
Is their problem.
Not yours to take on.
If they leave with no return...
That's okay.
They weren't meant to stay.
You can change.
You can grow.
If they can't accept that,
That is not on you.
Stop trying to fix others.
Stop catering to them.
Stop meeting their needs,
What about yours?
You have needs too,
Pay attention to you.
Stop playing the victim,
You played a role too.

You over gave and didn't speak up.
You over gave and left nothing left for you.
You didn't communicate what you needed.
You overstayed,
When you should have left.
You kept on forgiving.
Thinking about them.
Sacrificing yourself,
And only giving to them.
Not speaking your truth.
Afraid to rock the boat.
Afraid of a punishment.
Afraid to be scolded.
Afraid of disappointment.
Afraid to be abandoned.
Afraid to just be you.
Afraid to be who you really are.
This chameleon you became,
To meet their needs.
Bend to be who they need you to be.
Bend to fit in.
Bend to make them happy.
Making them happy is how you lived.
Putting them first,
Yourself last.
This became your life.
A walk, through codependency.
You have opened your eyes.
Your eyes are wide open now.
You see it all now.
You see it so clear.
This is not who you are.

This is not who you will be.
Walking away,
From codependency.
This is not where you belong.

Just Be

Let everyone live.
Live the way they want to live.
Let everyone just be.
Let them do their own thing.
Let everyone go.
Go do what they want to do.
Let everyone go.
Go be where they want to be.
Let everyone say,
Whatever it is that needs to be said.
Let everything play out,
The way it is supposed to play out.
Surrender to it all.
Surrender is the key.
Surrender with no expectations.
Surrender with no control.
Surrender and trust.
That is the key to it all.
Let everyone just be,
Whoever they want to be.
Let everyone live,
The way they want to live.
Let everyone be.
Let everyone just be.
Everyone just needs to be who they need to be.
Just be whoever you are.
Just be the person you want to be.
Just be that girl.
That girl you were always supposed to be.
Just be her.

No matter what.
Just be that girl.
You don't even have to try.
You don't even have to hide.
You just are her.
This is who you were always supposed to be.

Lose It All

Lose it all,
To fall in love.
Fall in love,
With yourself.
Lose it all,
It's worth the risk.
Lose it all,
To find yourself.
Lose it all,
To take the risk.
This risk of loss,
Brings you love.
This risk you take,
To discover your heart.
This risk you take,
To feel secure.
This risk you take,
Will have you full.
Fulfilled with love.
Love for yourself.
Lose it all,
To fall in love.
Fall in love with you.
You are in love.
Finally, you are in love.
In love with yourself.
This is the risk.
Lose it all.
Lose external love.
Lose conditional love.

Lose that transactional love.
This is all taking up room.
Taking up room from your own love
Lose the distractions.
Lose the noise.
Lose the plans.
Just lose it all.
Drop the weight.
Love is left,
At the end.
After this risk.
This risk you take.
It is worth the wait.
This wait was love.
This love for you.
This love for yourself.

Send It Back To You

Unconditional love.
I will love you,
Even from afar.
I will love you,
Even though you are over there.
I will love you,
Even though you are not in my life.
I send you love.
Love from a distance.
I send you love.
Love from afar.
I send you love,
Even if we parted ways.
I send you love,
Over your way.
I send you love,
Because we all are just figuring this out.
Figuring out this life.
How are we surviving,
In everyday life?
How are we getting by?
We get by with love.
I will send you love.
Love to where you are.
I will send you love.
The way you treated me...
It wasn't right,
But I forgive you and I love you.
The games you played with me,
I understand where they came from.

I send you love.
I can't be there.
I can't be with you.
I am over here…
But I still send you love,
From where I am.
I am here,
Finding forgiveness.
Finding forgiveness for you and for myself.
Finding love inside of myself.
Finding love for you,
To send it back to you.

Under The Stars

She was born to sit.
Sit under the stars.
Sit under the moon.
Sit under the sky.
Under the clouds.
Feeling the sun.
The warmth of the sun.
The sun on her skin.
She was born to sit,
Sit on the earth.
Sit on the grass.
Grounding herself.
Her feet on the ground.
She was born to connect.
Connect with the earth.
She was born to sit.
Sit by the water.
She was born to listen.
Listen to the waves.
The waves coming in.
The flow of the water.
It is all she hears.
Hours and hours go by.
She sits there for hours.
Nothing to do.
Nowhere to be.
Here she still is.
Sitting in stillness.
Taking this all in.
Taking in nature.

Taking in this moment.
This moment that is here,
As she sits on the ground.
This is who she is.
She sits under the sky.
She sits under the stars.
She could sit here forever.
Sitting in stillness.
Connecting with the earth.

We Liked You Better...

We like who you were.
Who you used to be.
Why did you change?
We don't like this new you.
Please go back.
Back to the way you were.
We don't know what to do.
What to do with the new you.
We don't want to hear.
Hear these new words you speak.
Speak these words of truth.
These honest words,
Out of you.
We liked you better when you hid.
When you made yourself small.
When you put us up on a pedestal,
Giving us praise.
Telling us how great we are.
We liked you better.
Better the way you were.
Because you made us comfortable.
You always made us feel good.
You did for everyone else.
You put us first.
We liked you better like this.
You were our lifter,
But we were not yours.
You exhausted yourself,
Just to make us feel good.
You gave your all away.

And that is what we liked.
We liked you better this way.
We liked you better when you stayed small.
It was easier to walk all over you.
It was easier for us to get our way.
We left filled up,
While you left drained.
We liked you better with no boundaries.
We liked you better when you did things our way,
And never thought about yourself.
We liked you better when you sacrificed yourself,
While meeting our needs.
We liked you better with a smile on your face,
While you were breaking inside.
We liked you better when you were always cheerful,
While your life was falling apart.
We liked you better when you stayed the same.
We liked you better when you did not grow.
We liked you better when you put us first.
We liked you better when you didn't talk back.
We liked you better when you didn't defend yourself.
We liked you better like that.
Because it is about us.
It is about what is good for us,
And really not about you.
We really don't think much,
About what is good for you.
We really only want what is best for us.
We liked you better when you stayed small.
We liked you better when we could manipulate you.
We liked you better when we had you on a leash.
We liked you better when you read from our script.

We liked you better when you were fearful.
We liked you better that way.
Because we could control you,
And you stayed small...
Right where you belong.
We don't like this new you.
This new you that has emerged.
We liked you better the way you were.
Can you just go back?
Back to that other girl?

Bait

Her freedom is her love.
This love for herself.
Her freedom is her trust.
Her trust in herself.
Her freedom is her faith.
This faith in herself.
Her freedom is her empathy.
This empathy she gives.
She gives to herself,
She will give it to you too.
She will give herself compassion.
She will share this with you.
She will nurture herself.
She will listen to her voice.
Her voice of intuition.
She will keep herself safe.
Safe in her own arms.
She will rely on her light,
To guide her down her path.
She will feel every emotion.
Every emotion she has.
She will not close her heart.
Not ever again.
She will live with her heart open.
Her heart is her beautiful place.
Her heart belongs to her.
Holding love inside.
Love inside for her.
To share with others on her path.
She has learned to share,

Instead of giving it all away.
She has learned the meaning of self-love.
She found her worth.
She has discovered her trust.
She has repaired her heart.
She has strengthened herself,
So that she can fulfill her dreams.
These dreams she has had,
For a very long time.
These dreams,
She shoved aside.
To meet everyone else's needs.
She was not aware,
Of any other way.
Until she discovered how many times,
Love was taken away.
Taken away to punish her.
Taken away to bring her down.
Taken away to fill her up.
Fill her up with wounds and hurt.
Love being held as bait.
Bait to her.
Bait as control.
She would chase.
Chase this bait.
This bait she knew.
She knew it as love.
This kind of love was all she knew,
Until she found this love in herself.
This bait no longer worked.
Worked as control.
She would walk away from this bait,

And trust in her love.
Trust in her light.
Trust in her heart.
Trust in herself.
Herself that she uncovered under all of the pain.
All of the wounds.
All of the tears.
Herself that she would never sacrifice.
Sacrifice, ever again.
Not ever, ever again for this bait.
This bait,
She knew as love.
This bait was no longer part of her world.
She left this bait behind,
As she found her new world.
This world that she walked into.
This world was hers.

Her Eyes

She sees with her eyes.
These eyes.
Her eyes.
She sees what no one wants to see.
She sees this clarity.
She sees this truth.
She sees this illusion.
This illusion of the world.
She sees with her eyes.
Her eyes,
They see.
Her eyes are wide open.
They cannot unsee.
They see what is real.
They see what no one wants to see.
Her mouth speaks.
Speaks words no one is ready to hear.
They don't want to hear.
Hear what is really going on.
Turn the blind eye.
Turn around to not see.
"No, don't look.
Just see what we want to see.
No, I don't want to hear.
Hear what you have to say.
No, don't look.
Just turn my back.
I will pretend I didn't hear what you just said.
Because I am not ready.

I am not ready to see.
I don't want to hear it.
Just close your eyes and stop.
Stop noticing all of this."
This is what they say.
But not her.
She walks right in.
Right in so that she can see.
She notices it all.
She sees it all.
She sees past the surface.
She sees what is underneath.
Underneath this illusion.
This illusion of the world.
Challenge this illusion.
This illusion of the world.
Challenge these beliefs.
Challenge what you know.
Challenge these responses.
These responses from the ego.
The control.
The defense.
The power.
The entitlement.
This instant gratification.
The fame.
The games.
This corruption.
This disfunction.
Scanning her environment.
She sees it all.

Her mask has come off.
So have the glasses.
The glasses that kept her from seeing what's real.
The glasses that kept her.
Kept her from the truth.
These rose-colored glasses.
They kept her safe.
She saw through a lens,
That had everything covered.
Covered with an illusion.
Covered with this lens.
This lens she looked through,
Until she didn't.
Until the day she no longer needed this lens.
She sees it all,
Just as it is.
As it is with no protection.
She now sees it all.
These defense mechanisms.
These coping mechanisms.
How people react.
This is how they react,
To her questioning this illusion.
She notices this.
She sees this.
She sees it all with her eyes.
Her eyes,
They know.
They know the truth.
Her eyes,
They cannot unsee.
Unsee this illusion.

Unsee this truth.
Unsee what her eyes have seen.
They just cannot unsee.

Manipulation

I see your manipulation.
I see it so clear.
Those words you say…
They are stringing me along.
Stringing me along,
To keep me controlled.
This power you hold.
You are manipulating me.
I do see it now.
I see it right away.
This tactic of control,
Because what I say makes you insecure.
Your manipulative ways,
To keep me where you want me.
Right where you want me,
Which is below where you are.
To keep me small.
You think I don't see?
You really don't think I see now,
What is really going on?
It took me a long time to see.
But now I see it.
Oh, so clear.
You want my reaction.
You want to play games.
You are thinking of yourself…
Only about yourself.
Ways to stay on top.
Ways to stay ahead.
I see all of this.

I also see your guilt trips.
I don't need this in my life.
I don't need this anywhere close.
Close to me.
I don't need this.
Your manipulative ways,
To keep you feeling good.
Oh, no thanks.
I am ahead of you.
You think I don't see.
You think I don't know what's really going on.
You think I'm naïve.
But I see this.
I see you,
Manipulating me.
I have collected tools.
Tools for this.
Tools for this tactic.
This tactic that you use.
I am ahead of you already,
Because I know just what to do.
I am watching you…
And I will remove myself so quick,
As soon as I see this.
My body will tell me when…
Don't worry,
This game you play…
It is coming to an end.

The Way Out

The way out.
Out of this cage.
This cage she was in.
In for so long.
She will fly free.
Free from that cage.
She will fly free.
She left that cage.
That cage kept her small.
That cage kept her.
Kept her from herself.
This cage,
She never belonged in.
Belonged in,
In the first place.
She finally found the key.
The key to this cage.
Her truth was the key.
The key to this cage.
This key freed her.
Freed her from this cage.
She grew her wings.
She earned her place.
She used her voice.
She found her freedom.
This key to her freedom.
Her freedom was the truth.
Finding the truth.
Speaking her truth.
Her truth.

Her story.
Her feelings.
Her love.
This key,
She holds.
This key she puts down.
She put it down finally.
Now that she is out.
Out of this cage.
She has left this cage,
And will never return back.
She is gone for good,
She will not look back.
She no longer needs this key.
This key to this cage,
That kept her locked up.
Locked up her whole life.
She found her way out.
She has left this cage.

Always Be... The Black Sheep

She couldn't have a reaction.
A reaction of any kind.
She couldn't have a reaction.
Any kind of reaction.
She couldn't have a response.
Her response didn't matter.
Her emotions didn't matter.
She couldn't react.
She couldn't come undone.
She couldn't unravel.
She couldn't get mad.
She couldn't get upset.
She couldn't be sad.
She couldn't cry.
Her feelings were shut down.
She was put down.
Put down so many times.
She was kicked down.
Down to the ground.
She stood out.
Stood out from day one.
She stood on her own.
On her own from the very start.
On her own,
Is what she knows.
This is what she knows.
Trying to fit in.
Trying to be loved.
Loved,
Unconditionally.

Loved,
Without conditions.
Trying to be a person she is not.
A person she had to be.
Had to be for them.
A person she gave up,
Because she is the black sheep.
She was not loved for who she was.
She was kicked down for who she was.
This was all because,
She was the black sheep.
The black sheep.
She is just on her own.
That is who she is.
She is and will always be,
The black sheep.

Done Keeping Secrets

I am done keeping secrets.
Secrets that weigh me down.
These secrets are yours.
I am done keeping these secrets.
These secrets for you.
These secrets I keep.
I do it for you.
I will release.
Release these secrets.
These secrets will set me free.
These secrets I've kept.
I've kept them in,
To protect you.
To protect your peace,
To let you look good.
I've kept it all in,
For your sake.
But what about me?
What about my peace?
I am done protecting you.
I am done.
I am done staying small.
I am done keeping it all in.
I am done.
I need to release.
Release it all.
Put it all down.
Remove it all.
Get rid of it.
Dropping this weight.

This weight I carry.
This burden.
This burden I took on,
To protect you.
But what about me?
Your secrets I have carried.
Your secrets I have kept.
I am giving them back.
Back to you.
Sending them all back.
Back to you.
These are not my secrets.
These are yours.
I did this to protect you.
But it is my turn now,
To protect me.
Vulnerability is the key.
Vulnerability will release it all.
The truth.
Honest and raw.
Put it all out there.
What I went through…
Here it is.
No more secrets.
No more hiding.
Hiding beneath this weight I carried.

What's The Matter?

What's the matter?
Am I rocking the boat?
Am I rocking your world?
Am I affecting your illusion?
This illusion you live in,
So that you feel big?
So that you feel superior?
So that you feel like you are on top?
What's the matter?
Am I affecting your pedestal?
This pedestal you stand on.
So that you are above me?
What's the matter?
Am I not giving you enough love?
Enough love,
Served on this platter?
This platter I stopped serving.
Serving to you.
This platter I took back...
To serve to myself.
What's the matter?
Am I affecting your mask?
Your mask you put on.
This mask you wear.
Am I affecting your façade.
This façade you put out.
Put out to the world.
Put out to show.
To flaunt.
Everything is for show,

In your world.
What's the matter?
Am I affecting your performance?
Your performance you put on.
Put on for your "friends."
Put on for the public.
Put on for the world.
You,
As the main character.
Them,
As your audience.
Them,
Buying tickets.
Tickets for your show.
The only way you make it,
Is if they keep buying tickets.
The show must go on...
So must your performance.
What's the matter?
Am I affecting your ticket sales?
Am I affecting your show?
Am I affecting your audience?
Is your audience getting smaller?
Does your audience know...
That this is all a performance.
A performance you put on.
Just to profit.
Profit from their payment.
Their payment for these tickets.
Does your audience know?
This is the only way you survive.
You survive because of them.

You survive because of this performance.
This performance you put on.
But what happens when it ends?
When this performance stops.
All things must come to an end.
What happens when it's the end?
What happens to you,
Then?
Not my problem...
Just thought I would ask.
For now,
I leave you.
To perform for your show.
Good luck to you,
As you perform for them.

The Fire Is Over

These blazing fires.
Everything is on fire.
Everything behind her,
Everything is on fire.
Everything is burning.
Burning away.
Everything is scorching.
Everything behind her,
It is all gone.
This blazing fire took it all away.
It is burned away.
Burned away to a crisp.
Burned away to nothing.
Now all there is,
Is smoke.
A smokey black haze.
This smoke fills the air.
This air behind her.
All that is there,
Is smoke now.
All that is there,
Is nothing.
Everything burned.
Burned to the ground.
Everything is gone.
Everything she knew.
This fire took it all.
What is behind her,
Is smoke now.

When the smoke clears away,
All that is left is nothing.
Nothing is there.
Time for a new beginning.
Time to start over.
She looks over her shoulder,
To see nothing is there.
The smoke is now gone.
She decides now,
To never look back again.
She will no longer look back.
Look over her shoulder.
This fire is over.
The fire is out.
The smoke is gone.
The destruction is done.
That chaos has stopped.
It is quiet now.
It is peaceful now.
She can look forward now.
The fire is gone now.
The smoke is gone now.
She can be calm now.
She can take a breath now.
Breathe in.
Breathe out.
Time to start over.

Why?

I see you.
Why am I seeing you?
Out of nowhere you appear.
You come when I am down,
I come when you are down.
I leave you,
And you always make an impact.
An impact on me.
An impact on my heart.
An impact on my soul.
Why does this happen?
What is this draw?
I am so drawn to you.
You are so drawn to me.
We are connected.
Connected somehow.
You leave my presence,
And I feel you still.
Why are you here?
Why did I see you?
Why did you just appear,
Out of nowhere?
Just today,
Out of nowhere.
There you are.
You ran away.
You ran away pretty quick.
You wouldn't stay.
This is probably good.
Good on your part.

Given our last conversation that we had.
I know you were uncomfortable,
Is that why you ran away?
I see your growth,
Just know that I see you.
I heard your words,
I read your vibe.
The vibe when you left,
I picked it up.
I picked it up,
I understand.
Just so you know,
I understand.
I love to be in your presence.
I want you around.
I love to hear you talk,
I love how you listen.
You listen to me,
You really listen.
You understand me,
You just get it.
You hold empathy.
Empathy for me.
You hold space.
Space in your heart.
Thank you for this space,
I am thankful.
Thank you for hearing me.
Thank you for caring.
Thank you for being a beautiful person.
This feeling...
This feeling,

You have it too.
You told me once,
And I feel the same.
Why did I see you today?
Are you a sign?
A sign meant for me?
Am I your sign?
A sign meant for you?
What is this sign?
Why did I see you?
You are a lifter,
And so am I.
Maybe we are just each other's lifters.

The Unknown

Leaving your comfort zone,
Brings this discomfort.
Leaving your comfort,
Brings this burn.
This sting.
This discomfort.
These uncomfortable feelings.
Nothing is the same.
This is so much change.
Leaving your comfort,
Will leave you burning.
Fidgeting.
Moving.
Nothing is at ease.
Everything is hard.
Everything is new.
Ask for some help.
You can't do it alone.
Leaving your comfort,
Will bring emotions.
Emotions you don't know.
Emotions that are exhausting.
You just want to sit.
Sit down.
Sleep.
You are exhausted.
Exhausted from feeling.
Feeling these emotions.
Moving into the unknown,
Without a clear outcome.

Moving into the unknown,
Without a clear answer.
You don't know how it will end up.
You don't know how it will go.
You are not in this alone.
This is the unknown.
You have support.
Put yourself out there.
Go for what you want.
Ask the questions.
The questions you want answered.
This is the unknown.
You have never been here before.
You are filled with discomfort.
Don't forget to listen.
Listen to your voice.
That inner voice.
Go for what you want,
And don't give up.
Go after that thing.
That thing that you want.
That thing that is outside.
Outside of your comfort zone.
Go into the unknown.
This is where you are headed.
This is where you belong.
Fill yourself up with love,
And stand tall.
This is what you want.
Do not give up.
Let yourself feel.
Feel this discomfort.

This discomfort is here.
Here to stop you.
Stop you from leaving.
Leaving what you know.
That discomfort is here.
It is here to be a roadblock.
This barricade that came to hold you back.
This fear is intense.
It fills you up.
The only thing that will stop it.
The only thing stronger.
Strong than fear...
Is hope and love.

This Gentleman

I see this gentleman.
This gentleman opens the door for me.
A normal door.
And the car door.
Opens the door,
And says, "I've got this."
I walk through the door,
With his hand on my back.
He is here to protect me.
He guides me.
He leads me.
He leads the way.
He decides the next place.
He makes the plan.
He makes the reservation.
He pays at the end.
He hangs up my picture.
He fixes the toilet.
He fixes each leak.
He helps in the yard.
He walks my dog.
He opens the door,
Once again.
I love this.
(I love when he opens the door,
Especially the car door.)
Thank you I say.
He needs to feel appreciated.
A gentleman deserves,
To feel appreciated.

He deserves respect.
He deserves my love.
He deserves to be told how great he is.
I love when he carries my purse!
(I know he doesn't really want to do that,
But he does it to make me happy.)
He wants to see me happy.
He helps me paint.
He helps with the house.
He helps with ideas.
He calls me out.
(Please call me out.)
He helps with decisions.
He is there to protect me.
He has my back.
He always drives,
With me holding his hand.
He won't raise his voice.
He won't yell at me.
When he is mad at me,
He knows what he needs to do.
All he needs to do,
Is come out with the truth.
Speak his mind.
Speak his heart.
I am here to hear him.
He listens to my stories.
He listens to me vent.
Please help me carry these bags.
Please help with the garbage.
Please help me when I am sick.
He even got the vacuum!

What is this?!
A gentleman with the vacuum,
Are you serious?
(He does carry your purse,
So, he must be the real thing!)
This gentleman I see.
He stands by my side.
This gentleman I see.
He would never tell me a lie.
He is honest with me.
He would never leave.
He is there to hear me.
He is there to listen.
He is there to see me,
And learn what I need.
He is there.
It is him that I trust.
It is him that won me over.
It is him in my heart.
This gentleman I see.
He is here to stay.
This gentleman I see.
He is rare.
He is so rare.
I have not met him yet.
I am waiting for him.
This gentleman.

This Freedom Came

This freedom that came,
When I walked away.
Away from what was not meant for me.
This freedom came,
When I turned inward.
Inward to my soul.
Inward to my heart.
This freedom came,
When I stopped.
Stopped taking on everyone's problems.
This freedom came,
When I started to believe.
Believe in myself.
Believe and trust.
Trust in myself.
Tune in fully.
I can only do so much.
I can only be.
Be who I am.
This freedom came,
When I stopped being.
Being what everyone else needed me to be.
This freedom came,
When I accepted.
Accepted me just as I am.
When I accepted life as it is.
It is what it is.
This freedom came,
When I stopped trying to fix.
When I stopped trying to change.

Change the situation.
Let people be who they are.
Let them see what they want to see.
Stop trying to force.
Stop trying to control.
Let everything just be.
Just be as it is.
This freedom came,
When I became.
Became who I was always meant to be.
This freedom came,
When I walked away…
Away from a world.
A world I didn't belong in.
A world that dimmed my light.
This freedom came,
When I stopped being,
At everyone's beckon call.
This freedom came,
When I learned the word no.
This freedom came,
When I put the platter down.
This platter I was serving to everyone else.
This platter I was serving to please everyone else.
This freedom came,
When I left that cage.
That cage I was in.
In for so long.
This freedom came,
When I took those rose-colored glasses off.
This freedom came,
When I stopped giving energy.

Energy to what isn't even happening.
Preparing for the worst.
Having my guard.
Putting up my armor,
Just to have an interaction.
This freedom came,
When I became myself.
My true authentic self.
This freedom came,
When I stopped everything else.
This freedom came,
When I listened to my body.
My body has been speaking all of these years.
My body has told me.
My body has led me.
This freedom came,
When I allowed myself to trust.
Trust in myself.
Trust in my body.
Trust in my heart.
Trust in my intuition.
This freedom came,
When I set it all down.
Set down the expectations.
Set down the plan.
Set down illusion.
Set everything down,
That isn't mine.
This is not mine.
Neither is this.
Keep moving forward,
As I don't look back.

Put my past behind me.
Nurture my wounds.
Embrace a new start.
Acceptance and forgiveness.
Opening my heart.
Loving myself,
Just as I am.

This Illusion

Take this illusion.
Take it away.
It wasn't what I thought.
Thought it was.
None of it was real.
It was all an illusion.
An illusion I made.
Everything I knew,
It was all a lie.
I couldn't see.
See the reality.
I kept myself safe.
Safe with this illusion.
I couldn't see,
Who they really were.
Using me to meet their needs.
Using me to fill a void.
A void inside of them.
I couldn't see,
Because I didn't want to see.
I had to be ready.
Ready to see.
I had no idea,
What love really was.
Because all I knew was,
Love as breadcrumbs.
All about them.
What suited them.
It was never about me,
And what I needed.

Throw me away,
Like I was nothing.
Come back when they need something.
Having these expectations.
Expectations of me.
If they do something for me,
I must do for them.
Expecting something in return.
What's in it for them,
What do they get?
Their needs matter.
Only theirs.
On their time.
No consideration.
No consideration for me.
No consideration for my feelings,
For my life.
Oh, this illusion.
I see it now.
I see it all now.
It wasn't what I thought.
Everything I knew,
It was all wrong.
Reteach myself.
Go find myself.
Put the illusion down.
That world is gone.
Find where you belong now.
Go where you belong.
It is your turn now.

Accept

Accept this illusion.
Just as it is.
Accept what life brings.
Accept that life is this.
It is what it is.
This is life.
Accept this as it is.
Acceptance brings peace.
Serenity and bliss.
Accept everything as it comes.
As it is.
Acceptance brings empowerment.
Empower yourself.
People are who they are.
Accept them as they come.
They are on their path.
You are on yours.
Accept what's not meant to be.
Accept what is.
Accept this moment,
As it comes.
Trust in yourself.
Trust in this process.
Trust and let go.
Accept it and live.
Your energy is yours.
Your energy is your light.
Your energy is your empowerment,
You have empowered yourself.
Accept yourself,

Just as you are.
You don't need more.
You are perfect as you are.
Just be here now,
In this moment.
This moment you are empowered.
Stay with this.
This empowerment came after so much pain.
Stay here now.
Stay with this.
This empowerment is your bliss.
Your serenity right now.
Let yourself be whole.
Be whole with your light.
Your light is your empowerment.
Your light is your soul.

This Ascension

Listen.
Are you listening?
Listening to this ascension?
Higher and higher.
Raising the bar.
Raising this frequency.
Can you hear?
This ascension is here.
Dissolving the illusion.
Dissolving the layers.
Dissolving the fear.
The guilt and the shame.
Dissolving what holds you back.
Holds you back from your light.
This rebirth is happening.
Happening to you.
This spiritual ascension has come to take you.
Take you away.
Away from what you know.
New energy for you.
Your new personality.
These words that you use...
You are no longer the same.
Spiritual energy fills your soul.
Higher vibrations for you to feel.
Your soul is here.
Nothing and everything.
All at once.
Pure awareness.
Light and love.

Complete presence.
Let go of the past.
There is no future.
All you have is now.
This ascension.
This love.
This light.
Higher vibrations.
Let them come.
Nothing is permanent.
Let it all come.
Let it all go.
Feel this flow.
This flow of ascension.

This Wildflower Blooms

This wildflower blooms,
In the midst of this field.
This wildflower sways.
Sways with the wind.
This wildflower is still.
Still in this field.
This wildflower,
Alone.
Alone in the rain.
Alone in the storm.
The storm is gone.
This wildflower remains.
Remains all alone.
All alone in this field.
This field of green,
Weeds and grass.
This field of beauty.
This stray leaf blows by.
Blows with the wind.
This wildflower stands.
Stands by itself.
This wildflower blooms.
Blooms in this field.
All by itself.
The only one blooming,
In this field full of weeds.
This wildflower blooms.
Blooms with the sun.
Blooms with the storms.
Blooms with the clouds.

Blooms with the rain.
This wildflower.
This beauty.
This beautiful bloom.
Radiantly colorful.
These hues stand out.
Stand out in this field.
This field of green.
These hues of light.
This bloom.
These hues.
This wildflower grows.
Grows with the weeds.
This wildflower.
Alone.
This wildflower blooms.

If You Could...

If you could say sorry.
If you could learn to say sorry.
If you could apologize.
Apologize for your actions.
If you learned accountability.
If you learned to take responsibility.
Responsibility for hurting the people.
The people in your life.
The people you have hurt.
We all make mistakes.
If you could learn to regulate your emotions.
If you could learn to be respectful to others.
If you could learn,
That your feelings aren't all that matter.
If you could learn,
To understand others.
If you could learn,
To consider others.
If you could learn to just be a decent human being.
If you could learn it is not all about you.
You aren't the only one,
The world doesn't revolve around you.
If you could learn...
Learn to say sorry.
Sorry goes a long way.
If you could learn to be humble.
Put your ego aside,
And apologize.
Conflict and repair.
It is so important.

Acknowledging your mistakes.
Acknowledging your flaws.
Allowing yourself to be vulnerable,
As you figure it out.
Put your shame aside,
And open up.
Put yourself out there.
Take that risk.
Let yourself be seen,
As you also consider me.
Put your ego aside,
It is not all about you.
Once you take accountability,
I will show you forgiveness.
But if you are shoving it aside…
Shoving it all under the rug…
Ignoring my feelings,
While you act like nothing happened.
Your actions are still the same,
Your behavior does not change.
I cannot do anything with that.
This blatant disrespect with no accountability,
Where am I supposed to go with that?
Your actions are consistent…
Consistent that they don't change.
Your lack of communication.
The meaningless words,
With no vulnerability.
What am I supposed to do with that?
Do you want me to chase you down?
Do you want me to fix it all?
Do you want me to figure it all out?

I am not shoving myself aside,
Not anymore.
I figured out that I matter,
I found my worth.
I am done being the one,
To always be the one to fix it.
The one to figure it out...
Figure it out for you.
I will keep moving forward,
As you fall behind.
This lack of self-awareness is holding me back.
It is not my job to show you.
That job is yours.
It is not on me,
To show you the way.
It is not on me,
To show you how to take accountability.
Your path may be different.
Different than mine.
And that is why,
I need to leave you behind.

Where Does She Go?

She is looking around.
Around at this world.
This world she is in,
Is just not for her.
Where does she belong?
Where does she fit?
It's not here anymore,
She knows this.
It's not here anymore,
She feels this.
This deep inner knowing,
Deep inside of her.
It comes every day.
Every day when she wakes up.
Every day when she opens her eyes.
Every day it is there.
This deep inner knowing,
It is always there.
Where does she go?
Where does she fit?
She is listening for the signs.
The signs to tell her.
She is open to hear.
She is open to see.
She is open for freedom.
This freedom is waiting.
Where will she go?
What is next?
She can feel it is not here.
It is just not here.

She doesn't belong here,
Not anymore.
She needs to get out.
Get out of this world.
She feels all alone.
All alone,
Where she is.
She doesn't belong here,
Not anymore.
She is this new girl.
This new girl that no one knows.
She is this new girl.
This new girl waiting for a new place.
She needs something new.
She needs to take a risk.
She is ready to jump.
She is ready for the plunge.
This new girl,
Needs to get out.
Get out of this world.
This world she is in.
This world is not for her.
Not anymore.
She feels like she is an outcast.
An outcast,
Looking in.
Not belonging.
Belonging to this world.
This world that she is in,
She needs to get out.
She is open and ready.
She will wait for the sign.

The sign.
The signal.
The next step.
It is not here yet.
She will know when she knows.
Right now,
She is just here.
Here in this world.
This world that she doesn't belong in.
Right now,
She is here.
Right now,
She observes.
She observes this world.
She sits quietly and watches.
Watches this world.
She sits quietly and asks.
Asks herself questions.
Writing to herself,
As she loves herself.
Bringing herself up,
To where she needs to be.
Where she needs to be,
So that she is ready.
Ready for what comes next,
Whenever that comes.
She will be in a good place.
Right now,
She is just in her quiet place.

This Quiet Place

This quiet place.
It is peaceful.
It is quiet.
It is so serene.
This quiet place.
Tranquil and calm.
Breathe in.
Breathe out.
This quiet place is hers.
This quiet place she is in.
She sits so patiently in this quiet place.
No noise.
No chaos.
No distractions.
No drama.
Just peace and serenity.
Solitude and freedom.
Her quiet place,
She made.
She made after the storms.
The storms and the fires,
That came to take her over.
The storms that came,
To take to her away.
The storms that came,
To disrupt her peace.
The storms that came,
To get in her way.
The storms that came,
To knock her down.

The storms that came,
That actually made her stronger.
The storms that came,
That brought her lessons.
The storms that came,
That made her who she is.
Who she is,
Today.
Who she is,
Right now.
These storms can't take her down.
She stood tall.
She found her peace,
As she found her strength.
She found her peace,
As she found her worth.
She found her peace,
As she found her love.
Breathe in.
Breathe out.
She found her peace.
She found her peace,
In her quiet place.

Trust In Herself

She will trust herself,
More than she ever has.
She will trust herself because...
Look how far she's come.
She's made all the decisions.
She has chosen.
She has made her choices.
These choices have led her here.
Here to where she is.
Here to where she is standing.
Here to this location.
This location,
Is where she is.
This location,
She reached.
Reached by trusting in herself.
Following her heart.
Listening to her inner guidance.
That inner voice has led her.
Led her to exactly where she is.
She will trust in herself.
She will believe in herself,
Because she is worthy.
Worthy of it all.
She will choose herself.
She has chosen.
Chosen herself.
This clarity is here.
It is her,
She trusts.

Not the outside world.
Trust is not found on the outside.
Trust is found.
Found in her heart.
How could she not?
Trust in herself.
Believe in herself,
This girl that she is.
This girl she has become,
By surrendering it all.
She is amazing.
These decisions she makes.
These choices she makes,
From her intuition.
Following her heart.
She finally sees herself.
With clarity,
She sees.
She sees this trust.
This trust she has built.
She is right where she belongs.
She belongs to herself.
Finally,
She trusts in herself.

You Will Figure This Out

When you have a direction.
This direction for you.
When you have a direction.
A direction you have to go.
This deep inner knowing.
This deep inner feeling.
This creeping feeling,
That will not go away.
It arrives each day.
This signal to you.
This silent sensation.
This very faint whisper.
"You have to go."
"You don't belong here."
You hear this every day.
You are listening.
You are in tune.
Your aura has changed.
People can notice.
It is no secret,
That you have changed.
You are not the same.
You are just not the same.
You have changed,
In so many ways.
You will not be taken advantage of.
You will not be used.
You will use your voice.
You will be in control.
Control of yourself.

You are in charge.
You have changed who you surround yourself with.
You embrace change.
You will not remain the same.
You know you must go.
Go somewhere new.
You just don't know when.
Where do you go?
You will figure it out.
You are listening.
You are in tune.
You will do what is best.
Best for you.
You will go to where you have to go.
You will figure this out.
Where do you belong?
You will hear a voice.
This voice within you.
This voice will tell you.
You are now done,
Dismissing this voice.
You now understand.
This voice is the leader.
The leader of your life.
The leader of your path.
The leader in your journey.
You will figure this out.

Her Way

She has found her way.
She found her way.
She has found her path.
She has discovered her way.
Her way is different.
Different than the norm.
Different than society.
Different than most.
Her way has come from hardship.
Hardship has changed her.
Her way was ruffled.
Ruffled with storms.
Ruffled with fire.
Burning through her life.
Her way had to change.
Change a million times.
Change until she got it right.
Change until she found her way.
Her way looks different.
Different than most.
Her way was disturbed.
Disturbed with pain.
Her way was disturbed,
Because she was on the wrong path.
She was going the wrong way.
She had to turn around.
Turn around to return home.
Home to herself.
She had to find a new way.
Changing everything,

Standing in her way.
Taking risks that many wouldn't take.
Facing her fears,
As she moved along.
Moved along on her path.
Finding her way.
Her way is different.
Different than most.
Her way is not understood.
Her way can be easily judged.
Easily judged because they can't understand.
But that's okay,
Because she found trust in herself.
She found trust in her ways.
She is okay with being different.
She is okay with going against the grain.
Going against what society says.
Going against what others say.
"No, thanks.
That is not my path.
No thanks.
This is setting me back."
Save money,
They said.
Put it away for the future.
You must think about the future.
She looks at them with confusion.
"The future is not guaranteed.
I don't live there,
In the future."
She lives in this moment.

This moment,
Right now.
Not in the future.
Right here,
Right now.
You must have a plan,
They said.
"But life doesn't follow a plan."
She argued back.
There is no plan.
There is no such thing,
As planning ahead.
You cannot predict the future.
You have no control.
Let everything go.
Live for right now.
Live for now.
Everything will end up,
Just the way it's supposed to.

Responsible

I am open.
Emotionally open.
I am trusting.
Trusting of myself.
I have learned boundaries.
I have learned not to be emotionally dependent.
Dependent on others.
I am responsible.
Responsible for my feelings.
I am responsible.
Responsible for my life.
I am responsible for what I allow.
I am responsible for what I put up with.
I have learned communication.
I have found my worth.
I found understanding.
Understanding for myself.
I have found compassion.
Compassion for myself.
I have found forgiveness.
Forgiveness for myself.
I have found my beliefs.
I have found my values.
I know what I want now.
I have set myself free.
Free from the burdens.
The burdens I carried.
Free from the hardships.
The hardships I endured.
I learned to reprogram.

Reprogram my beliefs.
The beliefs I had.
I had for myself.
I speak so kindly to myself now.
I have figured out how to empower myself.
I took my power back,
And never returned.
Returned to self-sacrifice.
Never again will I go back to that world.
I had to learn to love my little girl.
My little girl who lives inside of me.
I've learned to hold her and nurture her,
Anytime she needs.
It is no one else's responsibility.
I am responsible for what I allow.
And now what I allow,
Is empowering myself.

Taking You Off That Pedestal

Let me take you off that pedestal.
That pedestal that you were on.
Let me take you down,
Let me take you off.
Let me see who you really are.
You are showing your true colors,
Now that I have stopped lifting you up.
I was your lifter,
I didn't see your colors.
Your true colors,
Until now.
I am seeing so clear.
I understand.
I see what was going on,
All of those years.
I was sacrificing myself,
As I lifted you up.
Lifted you up onto that pedestal.
That pedestal that you were on.
You treated me like I was below you
And I thought this was normal.
I couldn't see it,
Not until now.
Because that was my whole life,
Holding people up onto their pedestals.
Giving my love,
All of my love.
Giving it all out,
Leaving nothing left for me.
Making everyone around me,

Feel worthy.
Using me,
To fulfill their needs.
Using me,
In this condescending way.
Talking down to me,
Like I don't know what I am doing.
Talking down to me,
Like you are better than me.
Talking down to me,
Like you know more than me.
Talking down to me,
Not allowing me to just be me.
Just let me do my thing,
Let me figure it out.
Figure it out on my own.
You think I need you,
And your opinions.
You think I need you,
To give me your advice.
Talking down to me,
Keeps you on that pedestal.
Until I take you off,
And I see it all.
I will no longer allow you to talk down to me.
I now understand,
That you are acting condescendingly.
I now understand,
That you think you are better than me.
I now understand that I am allowing this.
I will no longer allow this.
Allow this to go on.

I have let this go on,
For far too long.
This is all getting to be too much for me,
I need to put an end to this behavior.
This behavior that you are showing me.
I will walk away.
Walk away from this now.
I will no longer allow you to talk to me that way.
I will no longer allow you to behave this way.
I am walking away,
From condescending behavior.
You think you are better than me,
And that's okay.
You can think that,
As I walk away.

As It Is

This little girl.
This little girl inside.
This little girl lived in this illusion.
Lived in this illusion,
Her whole life.
Seeing the best in everyone.
Seeing the good.
She wants to see the good,
And only the good.
She would hold everyone up.
Everyone up on their pedestals.
She would make sure to make them feel good.
She would praise them and lift them up.
Give them love,
All the while she gave herself none.
Allowing everyone to walk on her.
Because she would understand,
Where it came from.
She understood what was underneath.
She understood what would drive this behavior.
She understood that they were hurting.
They were hurting,
Underneath this behavior.
She didn't love herself enough,
To stand up for herself.
She didn't believe she was worthy enough,
To be treated better.
All she would see,
Is that they were hurting.
All she would feel,

Is their emotion underneath.
Underneath this behavior.
She understood why.
Their pain.
Their insecurity.
Their fear or their shame.
She always could understand,
Why they were acting this way.
Her empathy & codependency,
Were getting in the way.
She really thought she was responsible,
To help them with their problems.
Shrugging off the blatant disrespect.
Shrugging off the mistreatment.
Shrugging off the projecting.
Putting herself aside.
Putting herself below them,
Putting herself at the bottom.
Forgiving and forgiving,
And giving out second chances.
Third and fourth and fifth and sixth.
Chance after chance,
She would give to them.
Maybe they just need more time.
Maybe they need me to help them.
Maybe if we have a conversation.
Maybe if I ask them questions.
Maybe they are changing.
Maybe they will realize.
Maybe they just need to see it.
Maybe they just don't know.
No.

This is not okay.
Even if they are in pain,
That is their problem...
Not hers.
She was worthy,
From the very beginning.
She just couldn't see it,
Because of how she was being treated.
She thought this was normal.
This kind of behavior.
This was familiar.
Familiar to her.
This is not okay,
The way she was treated.
She will stand up for herself now,
As she communicates her needs.
She will stand up for herself now,
When she is being put down.
She will stand up for herself now,
She will put them in their place.
Or she will decide,
To just take her words away.
They don't deserve her words,
She is just walking away.
Walking away from this mistreatment.
Walking away from the games.
She will not play them,
She will not participate.
Participate in the put downs.
She is done staying small.
She is done lifting you up.
She is done fixing problems.

Problems that are not hers to solve.
She is done explaining.
Explaining why.
She is done being scolded.
She is done being punished.
This little girl thought this was normal.
This little girl didn't know any different.
This little girl no longer lives in an illusion.
This little girl sees everything,
Just as it is.

Your Broom

It is what it is.
People are who they are.
Take it as it comes,
Let it go when it is done.
Accepting everything.
Everything as it comes.
Everything as it is.
It is what it is.
This illusion is gone now.
This situation is this.
Deal with it as it comes,
You have put your broom down.
You are done sweeping.
Sweeping it all away.
You are done with this broom,
It is finally set down.
This broom kept you from seeing what's real.
Sweeping and sweeping,
Until you were filled up.
Filled up with an illusion.
Filled up with dirt.
You could no longer see clear.
You were seeing through these piles of dirt.
These piles of dirt were affecting your vision.
These piles of dirt that you were given.
Some of it yours,
Some of it,
Theirs.
Piling more and more...
And more and more.

This broom needed to be put down,
A long time ago.
This broom kept you from yourself.
Piling everything.
Piling it all.
Piling everyone's problems on top of yours.
Just sweep this away.
Just get it out of the way.
Just move on.
Just keep holding this broom.
Holding this broom,
Until you put it down.
Putting it down now.
No more piles.
Dealing with it as it comes,
Because there is no broom.
This broom has been put away,
Permanently now.
Deal with each problem.
Deal with it as it comes.
Walk away from the people,
Who bring more dirt to sweep up.
Do not allow more dirt to come into your area.
Into your aura.
Into your field.
You are not responsible for everyone's dirt.
You are responsible for yours.
Your dirt,
And only yours.
Your dirt...
As it comes now,
You are done sweeping.

Let everyone else know,
You are done with the broom.
Everyone is so used to you,
Standing there with your broom.
Everyone is so used to you,
Cleaning up their dirt too.
Everyone is so used to you,
Allowing them to come dump on you.
Everyone is so used to you...
You with your broom.
You have replaced your broom,
With your voice.
The words you speak,
Will take care of the dirt.
The words you speak,
Will prevent the piles.
You have replaced your broom,
With your feet.
The steps you make,
As you walk away.
Walk away from the piles.
Walk away from the games.
Walk away from the dirt.
Walk away from the pileup.
Your broom has been put down,
So that you can use your feet.
Use your feet.
Use your voice.
Deal with it as it comes,
You are done with your broom.

The Story Of Your Grief

Grief will swallow you.
Swallow you up.
Grief will take you.
Take you over.
Grief is hard.
Hard to understand.
Grief comes and it goes,
You never know when it is coming.
Grief will hit you.
Out of nowhere,
It hits you.
Grief will keep coming,
Until you hear it.
Grief needs to be acknowledged.
Grief needs to be seen.
Grief needs to be heard.
Grief does not need to be dismissed.
Your grief comes,
To tell you a story.
Make sure to feel it,
Make sure to hear it.
Hear the story,
That your grief tells you.
Listen to the story,
Your grief shares.
Let your grief come,
Then let it go.
Feel this grief.
As hard as it is.
Feel this grief.

Let it come up.
Listen and feel.
Feel the sensations.
These sensations are here to flow.
Flowing and moving,
Don't let it stay stuck.
Body massage and energy work,
To keep your body open.
Keep your energy in your body moving.
Let the story of grief in,
And then let it go.
Tune in,
And listen.
Your grief will flow.
Flow throughout you.
Let it keep flowing,
And listen to the story.
Your grief will tell a story.
This is your story.
Your story of grief.

The Hardest Thing I Ever Had To Do

The hardest thing I ever had to do,
Ever in my life...
Was say goodbye.
Goodbye to you.
The very hardest thing I ever had to do,
Was close my heart off.
Close my heart off to you.
The very hardest thing I ever had to do,
Was to stop enabling you.
The very hardest thing I ever had to do,
Was take my heart.
Take it away from you.
The very hardest thing I ever had to do,
Was to become cold.
And give tough love to you.
Put my walls up,
Protect myself.
Show no emotion,
And walk around numb.
The very hardest thing I ever had to do,
Was to turn my back.
Turn my back to you.
The very hardest thing I ever had to do,
Was to detach.
Detach myself from you.
Turn my back.
Close my eyes.
Shut myself off.
Put one foot in front of the other.
Step by step,

As I walk away.
Walk away from you.
One foot in front of the other,
Trying to figure out a life without you.
One foot in front of the other,
Not knowing which way to go.
Go,
Without you.
The very hardest thing I ever had to do,
Was close the door on you.
The very hardest thing I ever had to do,
Was stop picking up phone calls from you.
The very hardest thing I ever had to do,
Was the day I had to give up.
Give up on you.
The very hardest thing I ever had to do,
Was realize it was not up to me to save you.
The very hardest thing I ever had to do,
Was accept that you were choosing you.
Choosing you,
And not getting help.
Choosing you,
And not our life.
The very hardest thing I ever had to do,
Was to understand that you could not see.
You could not see the beauty in you.
You could not see any other way out.
Ripping yourself to shreds.
Pulling yourself down.
Down to the ground.
The very hardest thing I ever had to do,
Was watch you destroy the you that I knew.

The very hardest thing I ever had to do,
Was to let go.
Let go of you.
The very hardest thing I ever had to do,
Was pick up the pieces of pain.
The pieces of pain,
Caused by you.
Each piece of my pain,
I picked up to feel.
I picked up to feel,
And I would see your face.
The very hardest thing I ever had to do,
Was to take it day by day.
Each day that went by...
Went by without you.
The very hardest thing I ever had to do,
Was walk away from you.
I had to walk away from you,
To save myself.
I had to walk away from you,
To love myself.
As I walked away from you,
I would pray so hard.
So hard for you.
Each morning, I woke up...
Sending hope to you.
Each morning, I woke up...
Having faith in you.
Praying for you,
To see your light.
The light that I know is inside of you.
The very hardest thing I ever had to do,

Was leave you...
Hoping you will someday find your light.
The very hardest thing I ever had to do,
Was put me ahead of you.
This lesson I learned.
I learned from you.
I am responsible for me.
You are responsible for you.
I am responsible for finding my light.
You are responsible for finding yours.
The hardest thing I ever had to do,
Was learn this lesson.
The hardest thing I ever had to do,
Was feeling my heart break.
My heart broke for you.
My heart broke for me.
My heart was just broken.
Shattered and broken.
The very hardest thing I ever had to do,
Was put it back together.
Back together again.
The very hardest thing I ever had to do,
Was heal.

The Big Picture

Just breathe through this.
Just breathe through it.
Just let it come,
And breathe through it all.
Breathe in.
Breathe out.
This feeling is here.
This feeling of anger.
This anger is here.
This is hard to feel.
So hard to feel.
Just breathe through this.
It will leave soon.
This anger is rising.
Rising through her body.
This anger is here.
She feels it in her eyes.
She is so angry,
That she was treated the way she was.
She is so angry,
She needs to let this come.
She is listening.
She is attentive.
She is paying attention.
She is aware.
She is aware now.
She sees all of this.
She sees this so clear.
It makes sense to her now.
But how had she not seen this before?

She let it go because she thought this was normal.
She let it go because this was familiar.
This is what she knew,
All that she knew.
She will never allow this mistreatment again.
She will never allow herself to be talked down to again.
She will not participate.
Participate in the games.
She is taking you off.
Off of that pedestal.
That pedestal she had you on,
For so many years.
She couldn't see you,
While you were standing up there.
Standing over her,
Like you were better than her.
She really believed you were better than her.
This is what you had her believing.
Treating her,
Condescendingly.
Talking down to her...
You liked her down there.
You liked her the way,
She was before.
You liked her better that way,
Because it was more comfortable for you.
You liked her better that way,
Because she was catering to you.
You liked her the way she was before,
Because she couldn't see who you really were.
She couldn't see because of this illusion.
This illusion she lived in,

And all that was going on.
Going on in her life.
Going on around her.
There was so much behavior,
That was just not okay.
So much that she let slide.
So much that she just let go.
She let it go because,
Why?
Why bring it up,
When you would tear her down.
Why bring it up,
When you would raise your voice.
Why bring it up,
When you wouldn't hear her words.
Why bring it up,
Because you were in control.
Why bring it up,
Because this was her role.
This role she was in,
For so long.
So many years,
She played that role.
The silent girl.
The passive one.
The easy going one.
The people-pleaser.
The girl no one saw.
The girl no one heard,
Because she didn't speak up.
She presented like she didn't care.
She presented like she shrugged it off.

She presented like she was okay.
She presented like nothing was a big deal.
This was because she was walking around numb.
Walking around,
Disconnected from herself.
Walking around,
Not knowing how she felt.
Walking around,
Being knocked down.
Being talked down to,
And she didn't even know.
She didn't even know,
Because this was the way.
This was the only way,
She knew.
Being talked down to,
And not being heard.
Begging for love,
Accepting breadcrumbs.
Breadcrumbs were the bait,
But only if she read from that script.
This script that they gave.
This script,
She knew well.
She knew it so well...
She knew how to act.
She knew how to act,
So, she wouldn't be scolded.
She learned how to act,
So, she wouldn't be left.
She learned how to act,
To keep everyone entertained.

She learned how to act,
To keep everyone comfortable.
She learned how to act,
To keep everyone happy.
She knew just what to do,
To keep them up on their pedestals.
Lifting them higher.
Lifting them up.
This was the way.
The way she knew.
Caring for everyone else,
While neglecting herself.
Shoving everything down,
Because who could she trust?
Being taught,
To always be the strong one.
Not being accepted,
As she figured herself out.
Having all of these expectations,
Put on her.
Meeting these expectations,
As her life fell apart.
Running around,
Doing.
Go.
Go.
Go.
Running around,
Trying to still be that lifter.
Running around,
With this smile on her face.

All while,
She just wanted to frown.
Trying to be there,
For everyone else.
Until the day,
She stopped.
She looked in the mirror and said,
"What??"
She started to listen to her inner voice.
She started to listen to that little girl inside.
That little girl needed to be cared for.
That little girl needed love.
She needed to make this commitment to herself.
She needed to figure herself out.
During this time,
She was not understood.
She was hurting others,
As she changed herself.
This was never her intention,
She feels badly about this.
But she needed to put herself back together again.
She needed to learn to put herself first.
She needed to believe in her worth.
She needed to see this big picture.
She needed to learn new ways.
She needed to reprogram herself.
She needed to figure herself out.
She needed to find peace within herself.
And once she found that,
It could not be taken back.
And once she found that,

The outside world didn't matter.
Once she found that,
Her whole world started to change.

Blind Spots

These blind spots in me.
These blind spots,
I could not see.
I could not see,
Because I was not going inside.
Inside of myself.
Inside of me.
These blind spots were created,
Because I was living outside.
Outside of myself,
In the external world.
These blind spots are there.
They are within me.
I will go inside.
Inside,
So, I can see.
Into my subconscious.
Here I am.
Here I am sitting.
Sitting in these blind spots.
These blind spots within me.
Oh my god,
Really?
It is so hard to see.
See myself.
This reality,
Of how I used to be.
It is hard to understand.
Understand myself.
It is so hard to look at.

Look at these parts.
These parts of me,
That I have kept hidden.
These parts of me,
That I have kept shoved down.
These parts of me,
Buried deep.
These parts of me,
That live within me.
These parts of me,
I have dismissed.
These parts of me that I need to acknowledge.
These blind spots have been created,
Because I didn't want to see.
I didn't want to see,
These parts of me.
I didn't want to know.
I wasn't ready to see.
I just wasn't ready,
I needed the tools.
I needed to get ready,
Ready for this.
Ready to see these parts of me.
These blind spots,
I will take.
I will take them in.
I will accept them,
And love them…
Just as they are.
No matter what,
I will love these blind spots…
Unconditionally.

Coming Off Her Pedestal

She needed to come down.
Come off of her pedestal.
Come off.
Step down.
Take her mask off.
Take away her mask.
That is not who she was.
Being this character.
Being that girl.
That girl needed to see her flaws.
Find her demons.
Find her blind spots.
Find her flaws,
As she learns to love them all.
Love those demons.
Love those flaws.
Make changes where she needs to,
As she finds herself.
Herself without her mask,
To be someone else.
She will be lost for a while,
Without her mask.
Without her mask,
Is who she is now.
She is lost.
She needs to find her way.
Get out of this cage,
And find her soul.
Without her mask,
She is not sure which way to go.

Her whole world on fire...
It is gone now.
Finding her way,
On her own.
Her heart is open,
and will show the way.
Her intuition will lead the way.
Listen closely.
Listen in silence.
Listen to this voice.
Her voice of intuition.
Her intuition is in charge.
She will surrender and trust.
So, she doesn't feel lost.
She will have faith and believe.
Believe in the change.
This change was needed,
For her to find her way.
Fires and storms came to take her down.
They take her down,
As she falls.
Falls down to the ground,
To find her tools.
Finding her tools to get her back up.
Learning and growing.
Discovering her way.
Her path is hard,
She will lower her guard.
Trusting in herself,
Because she now has the tools.
The tools she has needed,
To empower herself.

I Love You... If

I love you...
If you are the person, we want you to be.
I love you...
If you do as you are told.
I love you...
If you read from our script.
I love you...
If you stay the same.
I love you...
If you do not change.
I love you...
If you do not use your voice.
I love you...
Only if you are good.
I love you...
If you do for me.
I love you...
If you stay small.
I love you...
If you act like us.
I love you...
If you are fulfilling a need.
Fulfilling our needs.
I love you...
If you lift us up.
I love you...
If you serve your platter.
Your platter of validation and love.
I love you...
If you are down.

But only if you then do for me.
I love you...
If you shrug everything off.
I love you...
If you forgive us.
Forgive us for mistreating you.
Forgive us for leaving you.
Forgive us for projecting onto you.
Forgive us for punishing you.
Forgive us for using you.
All while you do not hold us accountable.
We will never take accountability.
We were not the ones who messed up,
It was you.
It was always you.
It will always be you.
We are never in the wrong.
It was always you.
We will pretend nothing happened.
Everything is fine now,
Because we swept it all away.
We can basically act however we want to,
And you just need to learn to accept it.
We will point out your flaws,
As we tear you apart.
Kick you down,
Harder each time.
We will never consider your feelings.
Because we only care about ours.
We don't want you to become better.
We definitely don't want you stronger.
We absolutely do not want you standing up to us,

Because we really enjoy giving you this conditional love.
We have conditioned you,
To act just the way we want you to.
So, if you change and become someone different,
This no longer benefits us.
We will still blame you,
Because all we know is I love you...
If.

Showing Up For Yourself

The way you say no.
The way you say yes.
The way you decline plans,
When you need rest.
The way you use your voice.
The way you communicate.
The way you walk away,
When it is time to walk away.
The way you give chances.
The way you forgive.
The way you understand.
The way you give compassion.
The way you set boundaries.
The way you respond.
The way you react.
The way you share your needs.
The way you speak up.
The way you live.
The way you care for others.
The way you care for yourself.
The way you spread love.
The way you show up.
Show up for yourself.
What do you need?
What can you learn?
When do you stop?
When do you go?
Are you listening to your body?
Are you connected to your intuition?
Do you spend enough time alone?

Are you recharging your energy?
Are you staying off your phone?
Are you eating the right foods?
Are you moving your body?
Are you in tune?
Can you hear your breath?
Are you meditating?
Are you feeling your feelings,
Or are you suppressing them?
Are you distracting yourself?
Are you acknowledging everything,
As it comes?
Or are you shoving it all,
Under the rug?
Do you go to therapy?
Are you being honest with yourself?
Can you take accountability?
Can you say sorry?
Are you running around on auto pilot?
Are you leaving your comfort zone?
Are you trying new things?
Are you going to new places?
Do you have hobbies?
Are you doing what you love?
Can you find what lights you up?
Are you surrounding yourself with noise?
Do you enjoy peace and quiet,
Or do you love crowds?
Do you like the busyness,
Or do you enjoy stillness?
Would you rather have music,
Or sit with no sound?

What are your passions?
Are you creative?
Do you enjoy reading,
Or would you rather see a movie?
Are you attracted to water,
Or would you rather sit on the grass?
Would you rather be at the beach,
Or walking on a hiking path?
Would you rather be hot and sweating,
Or be cooler wearing a sweater?
Do you want to go out and dance,
Or just sit at home?
Do you want to go out for drinks,
Or just be alone?
Do you want to be adventurous and travel,
Or just stay local?
Do you have the right friends?
Are you in the right relationship?
Are you growing?
Are you happy?
Do you need to make changes?
Can you support yourself financially?
Are you making enough money?
Are you living the life you want to be living?
Are you checking in?
Checking in with yourself?
How are you showing up?
Showing up for yourself?

I Held On...

I held on because that was all I knew.
I held on so tight because what was I going to do?
What was I going to do,
Without you?
How do I let go?
Let go of you.
Let go of it all.
When that was all I knew.
I built this life.
I had this love.
This love was attached to this life.
Letting it all go,
Was to go into the unknown.
I held on so tight,
Because I had hope.
I had so much hope.
Hope for you.
Hope for me.
I held on so tight because that was my whole life.
I held on so tight,
Because how do I let go?
How do I let it all go?
When that was all I knew.
How do I let it all go,
Because who am I now?
How do I let it all go?
That was who I was.
Let go of that hold,
As you go into the unknown.
Into the unknown,

All alone.
Into this unknown.
Feeling this grief,
Into the unknown.
Carrying this pain.
A choice I must make,
To feel this pain.
This loss.
A loss.
This loss came from love.
So much love I had for you.
I am letting it all go.
Drop this illusion.
This illusion I lived with.
I am letting it go.
This is no longer serving me,
As I more forward.
I need to let this go,
It is time now.

Give It Up

Her heart broke open,
As she saw it all.
Her heart was shattered,
As she saw the betrayal.
Her heart gave out,
As she grieved it all.
She let go of every, single thing she ever knew.
Give it up.
Let go and trust.
Finding her light,
Underneath it all.
If she hadn't let go,
She never would have known.
Known what was underneath.
Underneath her pain.
She never would have found,
This girl she is now.
She never would have found.
Found her light.
Her light.
Her love.
This path for her.
Her intuition guides her down...
Down this path,
As she holds onto faith.
She accepts it all,
As it comes.
She let go of hope,
To gain a clarity.
This clarity for her.

It was always there.
She just couldn't see.
Her pain,
In the way.
She needed new beliefs.
She needed to feel safe.
She needed to create a new world.
Create her inner world,
To go find her outer world.
Her inner world needed to change.
Her inner girl,
Needed to be healed.
She needed silence.
Peace and serenity.
Solitude and quiet,
As she left the noise.
She needed to repair.
She needed to mend.
She desperately needed to nurture herself.
Learning new ways.
Loving herself.
Learning,
To always empower herself.

Life

Create a community.
A community of love.
Create friendships.
Friendships that flow.
Create a foundation.
A foundation that will move.
Move with the changes.
The changes life brings.
Create an inner world,
Strong enough to take on the storms.
The storms that come along.
But soft enough to love.
Love through it all.
Create an energy that is vibrant,
That people open up.
Create an energy that you take care of.
Do not give it all away.
Create a self-awareness,
That you tune into every day.
Create yourself as a magnet.
A magnet of attraction.
Make sure to speak kindly.
Kindly to yourself and to others.
The words you speak have power.
Let them speak loudly.
Ask the hard questions.
Challenge it all.
Challenge everything.
Challenge what you know.
Let go of the labels,

Black and white thinking.
Do not let yourself be walked on.
Do not let yourself be talked down to.
Your psyche is important.
Treat it with care.
Take those risks.
The risks that fill you with fear.
The risks that make you uncomfortable.
Have the conversations.
The deep conversations.
The hard conversations.
Know yourself well enough,
To know when you are being triggered.
Feel your emotions.
Regulate yourself,
So that you are not projecting out.
Projecting your emotions onto everyone else.
Are you suppressing your emotions,
Or are you just avoiding them?
Are you acknowledging all of them,
Or are you dismissing them?
Have respect for yourself...
Always, every day.
Care for your body.
It is all you really have.
Learn what lights you up.
Do what makes you happy.
Find your passions.
Listen for your dreams.
The dreams that come along the way.
Keep your heart open.
Love unconditionally.

Walk away when you are done.
Stay when you want to stay.
Let everything be,
Just as it is.
It will all make sense someday.
Until then,
Just live your life.
Stay in each moment.
Each moment as it comes.
Do what you want.
Speak up.
Use your voice.
Set the boundaries.
Stay on your path,
Without looking back.
Listen to your intuition,
As you trust in yourself.
Your intuition knows it all.
Be open to learn.
Be open to love.
Get rid of expectations.
Work on your acceptance.
Accepting it all,
Just as it is.
As it comes.
Drop the illusion,
You don't need it.
Watch and observe.
Drop your control.
Live in discomfort.
Leave your comfort zone.
Try new things.

Learn to be vulnerable.
Give up being liked.
Know…
Not everyone will be happy.
Happy with your choices.
Your choices are yours…
So are your problems.
Lose your judgment.
Your judgment of others.
Drop the grudges.
Forget the resentments.
People are who they are,
Because of what they've been through.
Do not become bitter,
At those who hurt you.
That has nothing to do with you.
Fall down,
But get back up.
Always get back up.
Turn the ugliness into beauty.
Become your authentic self,
And love her more than anything else.

Judging...

Why don't you learn about me?
Before you criticize me.
Why don't you take the time.
Take the time to understand.
Ask me questions...
Why I am the way I am.
Before you judge me.
Before you try to fix me.
Before you make me your project,
And talk about my life behind my back.
You could get to know me...
You could try to understand.
But you don't.
Because you would rather criticize me first,
And have something to talk about.
Point out my flaws.
Make me your topic of conversation,
So, you don't have to look at yourself.
People are the way they are...
Because of what they have been through.
So why don't you open your mind,
And try to understand.
Put your criticism away.
I am not your project.
You don't need to pity me,
I have accepted what happened.
I power through,
As I find acceptance.
There is no quick fix,
Or instant gratification.

This is a long process of acceptance.
The only way out is through.
Letting go of it all.
If you are not here to help…
Help me as I fall.
I don't need your constant criticism.
I don't need you to point out my flaws.
I don't need to become your project.
This is not helpful at all.
It's fine if you want to judge me,
I just won't be around.

The Only Way I Knew

I stayed,
When I should have left.
I gave,
When I should have spent time by myself.
I stayed quiet,
Just to keep the peace.
I put myself aside,
When I should have come first.
I gave so many chances,
Because I thought that's what forgiveness was.
I put up with disrespect,
Because I thought that's what love was.
When I should have moved on,
I kept wishing.
Wishing for a change.
I kept trying to fix,
Because this was my role.
I allowed the manipulation,
Because I couldn't recognize it.
I allowed the put downs,
Because this was just normal.
Normal to me,
Because of what was surrounding me.
It wasn't until I took myself away.
Put myself into silence,
And it all made sense.
I opened my eyes,
To notice the world.
I needed to pay attention.
Pay close attention.

I needed to observe.
Observe the world.
What I knew was abuse,
And I never even knew.
Because that was the way…
The only way I knew.

On Display

On Display,
Like a show.
I am their object,
To make them feel good.
Someone different while people were watching.
Someone different while on display.
Painting this picture for everyone to see.
(Used to be me.)
Hard to see,
This in myself.
I did what I was taught.
This was my world.
Putting up this façade,
While wearing a mask.
This was the known.
The familiar.
I did this until...
The day I stopped.
The day I saw.
This realization.
This epiphany.
Oh my god.
Everything needed to change,
Mostly myself.
I needed to believe in my worth.
I needed to understand.
Understand myself.
As I changed,
I would lose.
Lose everything I ever knew.

Not going back,
To who I used to be.
That wasn't even me.
Everyone upset.
Everyone sad.
Sad for losing the me that they knew.
That me…
I needed to grieve.
That me,
I would have to lose…
To be the me that I am now.
Grieving that old life.
Grieving it all.
Losing myself,
And all that I knew.
Not who I wanted to be,
Not at all.
Even If I didn't want to lose her,
I had to let go.
Leaving it all behind.
Keep moving forward.
So much grief.
Letting it go.
Find me.
Finding myself.
And learning to love.
Love each part of me.
Even the parts,
That are so hard to see.
Loving and trusting.
Accepting and forgiving.
Believing and seeing.

Going through the darkness,
To find my light.
Collecting the tools.
Learning the lessons.
Do not give up.
I have come this far.
Keep on going.
My light,
I will hold.
I will be holding my light,
Soon enough.
I have always been light,
I just couldn't see.

Cheers To Me Now

This is for all the times.
All the times I did not speak up.
All the times I kept my mouth shut.
All the times I didn't stand up for myself.
All the times I made myself small.
Here's to all the times I was controlled.
Here's to all the times I was put down.
Here's to all the times my words were not heard.
Here's to all the times I was ignored.
Here's to all the times my voice was dismissed.
Here's to all the times I was not cared for.
To all the times I was used.
To all the times I felt like I didn't matter.
To all the times that everyone mattered more than me.
Here's to all the times I was shoved away.
To all the times I made a mistake...
Then was thrown away.
To all the times I was scolded.
Punished and demeaned.
Shamed and blamed.
To all the times,
I was betrayed.
Cheers to me now,
For seeing it all.
Cheers to me now,
For walking away.
Walking away from the games.
Walking away from everything thrown back in my face.
Walking away from where I no longer fit.
Walking away from what is not for me.

Cheers to me now,
For speaking up.
Cheers to me now,
For healing myself.
Cheers to me now,
As I empower myself.

This Space Of In Between

This space of in between.
In between my scars,
And what is about to start.
This space of in between.
This transition.
This transformation.
This space of in between.
Letting go of my past,
And opening my heart.
This space is for me,
To see the illusion.
That illusion where I lived.
Lived my life.
This space of in between,
Of losing what I knew…
And going to where I feel.
Where I feel aligned.
Where I feel alive.
Where I feel like me,
Where my soul will reside.
This space of in between,
Of being where I don't fit…
And going to where I fit in.
This space of in between,
Where I have disconnected…
And going to where I feel the connection.
Detaching from my scars,
And finding my love.

Detaching from what I know,
To go into the unknown.
This space of in between,
Is this lonely place.
This lonely place that only I know.
This lonely place where I must let go.
Let go of everything.
Everything I know.
This lonely place where I don't feel seen.
I don't feel seen because who am I here?
This lonely place where I am not understood,
Because I am around people who are living their life.
Right where they belong.
Right where they want to be.
Where they feel loved.
Where they are aligned.
Aligned with their life.
Their life they chose.
They are right where they belong.
I am right where I belong too…
I need to be here,
In this space of in between.
I need to be here,
Before I can leave.
Get it together,
Heal my wounds.
Prepare to be the girl that I choose.
This is my turn now,
To be that girl.
But first I must commit to this space.
This space of in between.
This loneliness.

Stay here now.
Stay right here.
I am right where I need to be.

Shine

I have given up anything external.
Anything external,
Cannot affect my worth.
The doing.
The going.
The succeeding.
The succession.
The accomplishments.
The making more money.
More.
More.
More.
Financial succession.
Financial achievement.
The competition.
How much do you make?
How much do you have saved?
The control.
Control of the money.
Control of the future.
Living in this lack.
It's not enough.
Not enough money.
This mindset.
Let it all go.
Let go of control.
The control of anything.
Anything external.
You don't have control.
Control of anything.

You have control of your body,
And that is it.
You can't predict.
Predict the future.
So why have a plan?
A plan for the future.
Let go of the plan.
All we have is this moment.
All we have is right now in this moment.
Right now.
Right here.
Just be here.
Just be in this.
Be in this right now.
Let go of everything else.
None of it matters.
Yourself.
You.
Your worth.
Your love.
Keep this and let the rest go.
The past.
Let it go.
The future.
Let it go.
Anything external.
Let it all go.
The journey is yours.
Own it and love it.
Surrender and trust.
This light you found.
You just need to hold it.

Your light will shine,
No matter what.
You don't have to do anything.
Anything at all.
Your light will shine.
Shine so bright.
Do nothing at all,
And your light will shine.

This Wildflower That She is

This wildflower that she is.
This wildflower is free.
The only flower like this.
Uniqueness is her gift.
So unique.
Standing out.
Standing out from the rest.
This wildflower.
She grows in the rain.
She blooms in the storms.
She lasts through the hurricanes.
She survives the earthquakes.
She rests in the sun.
She soaks it all in.
She blows with the wind.
Wherever the wind blows her,
Is where she ends up.
Adapting to her environment.
Whatever comes.
Never knowing what is coming.
She will just adapt.
This wildflower is blooming.
Radiant colors.
Beautiful hues.
Standing tall,
After the storms.
Surviving after she falls.
Her roots are strong.
They keep her grounded.

This wildflower blooms.
This wildflower alone,
Changes the world.

Deserved Better

I always deserved better...
Better than what I got.
I always deserved better treatment.
I deserved to be treated better.
I deserved the best,
And that is not what I got.
I deserved love,
Unconditional love.
I deserved to be held,
That's what I deserved.
Held when I was hurting,
That is what I needed.
I deserved to be heard.
My voice deserved to be heard.
I deserved to be seen.
I am a person.
A person with needs.
I did not deserve to be shoved away.
Shoved away to the side.
I at least deserved an apology,
One that came from taking accountability...
I deserved someone taking responsibility...
But now I know,
That person is me.
I am responsible for healing this hurt.
I am responsible for loving myself.
I am a person with a heart.
A heart that needed love.
I deserved to be understood.
That is what I deserved.

Cared for and respected.
I did not deserve to be walked on.
I should have never been a punching bag.
A punching bag to those I loved.
I always understood them,
And where it came from.
So, my heart kept forgiving.
Because I knew they were hurting.
But what about me?
I was hurting...
And I shoved myself aside.
Because that is what I was taught.
Shove her aside,
When she makes a mistake.
Shove her aside,
When she comes to you with the truth.
Shove her aside,
When she tries to help.
How am I not bitter?
How am I not cold?
After what I have been through,
How can my heart still love?
Because I understand.
I understand they were hurting.
I still understand that.
It does not make it right,
But I now know how to give myself love.
I will hold myself now,
And fill myself up with love.
I will heal these wounds,
And turn them into scars.
Scars that prove that I deserve the best.

The best came from me.
I will not allow mistreatment,
Ever again.
Not ever again.
I deserved respect.
I deserved to be kept.
I deserved to be held close.
I always deserved the best...
It is just not what I got.
I got what they could give,
And now I just need to learn to forgive.

Walked Away

You knew you had to walk away,
To connect to your soul.
Walk away from it all,
All that you knew.
Your soul called.
You followed it.
You listened,
As you walked.
Walked away from it all.
You walked away,
To walk towards the life.
The life that was waiting for you.
You found your gifts,
As you walked away.
You put everything down,
As you walked away.
You left your mask.
You left the façade.
You left the illusion.
You left the problems.
You left the emotions.
You left the pieces.
The pieces of your heart.
You picked them all up,
As you walked away.
You mended and repaired,
Each piece of your heart.
You put it back together...
Just to open it again.
You let go of who you were,

As you walked away.
Felt it all,
As you walked away.
Cried so many tears,
As you walked away.
You put yourself back together.
Back together again,
Differently this time.
A whole new you.
This is your soul.
No one knows,
This you that you are.
This you that you are,
This is the you that you became.
You became her,
As you walked away.

Dipping A Foot In

Let everyone move.
Move at their pace.
Let everyone go.
Go at their own pace.
Moving slow.
Not moving fast.
Not jumping in.
Dipping a foot in,
Just little bits at a time.
Let them think.
Process and decide.
It is something that takes time.
A process.
Everything is a process.
Just enjoy the moment.
No expectation.
No time frame.
No pressure.
Just let everyone be,
The way they need to be.
Let everyone go,
The way they need to go.
Let everyone just flow,
The way they need to flow.
Let it all just be...
Be whatever it'll be.
It will end up,
The way it ends up.
Trust and surrender.
Everything goes just as it should.

Let go of expectations,
And let it just play out.
Communication is important,
Because it lets them know.
It lets them know,
What you are thinking.
Communication is important.
Vulnerability is too.
Be honest and let people know.
Know what is going on.
Communication is a skill to be learned.
Learn it as you move along.
Move along through this life.
Learning as you go and letting everything just be.

Drifting Away

It's okay to drift away.
Drift away from the world.
Drift away to yourself.
Drift away,
To visit with your soul.
Drift away to your inward world.
It's okay to drift away.
Drift away when you need to.
Drifting is a part of life.
Everything changes.
Life is a drift.
Coming and going.
Drifting and flowing.
Letting it all come,
Letting it all go.
Life is drifting.
Drifting,
As we go.
As we flow through our life,
And figure ourselves out.
We change as we go.
Our experiences shift.
Our needs are shifting,
Constantly...
They are shifting.
Figuring out our needs,
As we go.
Life is a drift...
We can either go with it,
Or fight it.

Fighting it is controlling it.
Remove the control,
And surrender yourself.
Just let it be,
Whatever it is.
This comes with experience.
Learning as you go.
Holding on so tight.
Let go of the grip…
So, you can be someone new.
Let go of the grip when you need to.
Let go of that grip.
Letting go brings freedom.
Freedom brings serenity.
Serenity brings peace.
Peace for your soul.

...Not A Bad Thing

Crying is not a bad thing.
Crying is a release.
A release of what is inside.
Crying is a release.
A release of emotion.
An emotion you are feeling.
Crying is a release.
Crying is a goodbye.
Goodbye to the old.
Goodbye,
I don't need you.
Please let me cry,
Feeling sad is not a bad thing.
Feeling sad is okay.
Knowing what you feel.
Knowing what you need.
Feeling mad is not a bad thing.
Anger needs to come out.
It is what you do with it.
Have an outlet for your anger.
Anger doesn't need to be fixed.
It's okay to be angry.
Let me just be in this.
Let everyone just be,
In their own emotion.
Their emotions are okay.
Their emotions are theirs,
And mine are my own.
It's okay to cry.
It's okay to feel sad.

Anger is okay.
It all needs to be felt.
Let it all come.
Do not shove down.
Do not be alarmed,
If I am feeling an emotion.
I just need to be here.
This is where I am at.
And this is all okay.
Letting everything just be.
Just be as it is.
Drop the labels.
The good.
The bad.
Drop it all.
Is it really bad?
Compared to what?
What makes it good?
Labels aren't necessary...
Everything is,
As it is...
And that doesn't make it a bad thing.

Nothing Can Phase You

Lose the expectations.
Lose the plans.
Lose the control,
As you move along.
Lose it all,
As you let it go.
Lose the façade.
Lose the illusion.
Move along,
As you find your way.
Finding your beliefs.
Finding where you fit.
Disconnection brings detachment.
Detachment from a life.
A life that is over.
Everything you built.
All the love you gave...
It comes to an end.
The end is here.
Be realistic.
Be honest with yourself.
Everything you built came crashing down.
The attempts to love.
The attempts to try to fix.
Fix and change,
A dynamic that is not yours to change.
That life you built.
Let it go.
It is not for you,
You feel it in your soul.

You feel it in your bones.
You feel it every day.
You feel it in your heart,
As you tune in.
Everyone else,
Building their life.
Building up their life,
As you let yours go.
You built your life.
You built it with love.
Now you must let this love go.
This breaks your heart,
As you let it all go.
Who you used to be…
Let her go too.
You are no longer her,
As you grieve yourself.
Grieve that girl.
That girl you were.
That girl lost her passion,
As she lost her life.
In this process,
You found your tools.
These tools you need,
To let it all go.
Letting it all go,
Is so easy now.
Nothing can phase you,
As you just let it all go.

My Letter To You

You were my guy.
My one.
My love.
My life.
Watching you,
Deteriorate.
I can't even describe,
What that was like.
I couldn't breathe.
I could barely stand.
I shut my eyes,
I turned my back.
I walked away...
It was all I could do.
I couldn't stand it,
Watching you.
Watching you,
As you fell.
Fell so fast.
Fell into the dark.
Your heart,
So large.
Your beautiful heart.
I will always remember the love you gave.
The love inside of you,
It is still there.
The love inside of you,
Hasn't left.
The love inside of you,
Is waiting for you.

Waiting for you to wake up and see.
See that beauty.
That beauty in you.
That beauty in you,
Is not gone.
That beauty in you,
Is still there.
That beauty in you,
Is waiting for you.
Waiting for you,
To wake up and change.
The drugs you take,
Hide this light.
This light is in you,
I promise you.
These drugs are dimming.
Dimming your light.
These drugs are hiding.
Hiding your light.
Your light is there,
I am telling you it's there.
Your heart is huge,
Fill it with you.
Stop filling it with drugs.
Please,
Just stop.
I pray every day,
That you find this light.
This light in you,
That I know is still there.
This heart in you,
That needs to be cleared.

Cleared and renewed.
Attended to.
Your heart needs to be held.
Be held by you.
I will never give up.
Give up hope for you.
I still send you strength,
For you every day.
I still cry for you,
Because I have this hope for you.
I send you power.
Power for you.
You hold the power.
You are the only one.
The only one who has control.
Control over this.
Control over you.
You are the only one,
Who can wake up and say...
"I deserve to live.
I deserve to love.
I deserve to become,
My light inside.
I am worthy.
I know I am.
It is time for me.
A new me.
It is time to face...
Face my pain.
I believe in me,
I believe I can."
It has to be you.

Don't give up.
It is never too late.
Too late for you,
To say these words.
Wake up and say…
"Today is the day.
My new start,
Begins today."
I have hope.
I still believe.
I still believe you can do it.
I pray for this,
Everyday.
I pray for you,
Everyday.
I send you this,
Wherever you are.
This letter to you.
My letter to you.

...You Always Have Been

I believe in you,
I still do.
I believe you can do it,
I know you can.
I send you strength.
You know you have it.
Deep down you know.
You just have to see it.
You have to open your eyes.
You have to believe it.
Believe it in your heart.
Believe in yourself...
That you can do it.
You can find your light...
You just have to go inside.
Everything you need,
It is all inside.
I know you are a fighter,
Deep down.
I know you are not a quitter...
So why quit now?
You have been choosing to quit life,
Over and over.
You are making this choice,
Again and again.
Reach out for help,
If you don't know how.
You will figure it out...
How to make a new choice.
Drop down to your knees,

And believe in yourself.
Believe in God.
He will be your strength.
He will be your power,
Your endless support.
He will be there to hold you.
Hold you in the storms.
Hold you when you feel like you are not enough.
Hold you when you are falling apart.
He will hold you,
No matter what.
He will guide you.
Guide you to your worth.
He will guide you.
Guide you to your light.
He will bring you.
Bring you right to your love.
Your very own love,
That you are keeping covered up.
Covered up with those drugs.
Covered up with distractions.
Covered up with the noise.
You just have to believe.
Believe in yourself.
Believe in Him.
Don't ever lose faith.
Don't drop your hope.
Don't forget to grab your strength,
As you take care of this.
Take care of YOU.
I know you can do it.
I have never lost hope.

I send you this prayer,
To wake you up.
You are going to see...
You will have to feel some pain.
You will have to face your demons.
You will have to hold yourself.
You will have to prepare.
Prepare to go into the darkness.
It will be dark for a while,
But your light is your reward.
Your light will be waiting.
Waiting for you.
Your light is in YOU,
Calling you.
Open your eyes...
And see what I see.
You are worth it.
...You always have been.

I See You, Sadness

I see you, sadness.
I know you are here.
I feel you, sadness.
I feel you creeping in.
I see you and I hear you.
You come almost every day.
I know you, sadness.
You are grief.
I know you well,
From having so much loss.
I know you well,
You come with each goodbye.
I know you well,
You come as I walk away.
Walk away from what's not for me.
I welcome you, sadness.
I promise to honor you,
As I release.
I understand you, sadness.
I know why you are here.
I understand and honor you,
As I let you go.
I acknowledge you, sadness.
Each time you come.
I hold you, sadness.
As I cry my tears.
I support you, sadness.
As my grief reappears.
I give you a safe space,
For you to come.

As time goes by,
The less intense you are.
As time goes by,
The smaller the waves become.
As time goes by,
The easier it is.
Grief doesn't go away…
It lives inside.
Inside of me.
Because of the loss.
All of the losses brought you to me.
I know where you come from, sadness.
You come from my love.
The love I gave.
The love I shared.
You came from my love.
When my love realized,
It had nowhere to go.
I understand you, sadness.
I totally understand.
The more grief I have,
Is love that I had.
The love that I had for what I lost.
I welcome you, sadness
I know why you are here.

One Step At A Time

I go with the flow.
Wherever I go...
I go.
One step at a time.
Wherever I end up,
Is where I will be.
I will accept it as it comes,
And just surrender.
Loosen my grip.
Let go...
Not holding on.
Holding on so tight.
My grip is soft.
I go with the flow.
Sometimes I feel close.
Sometimes I let go.
This is life.
Life is changing.
Constant change.
Let go of control.
It is what it is.
Lose the expectations,
And let everything just be.
People are who they are.
They have their flaws.
Accept the flaws.
Accept mine too.
Own it all.
Unconditional love.

This rollercoaster ride.
The ups and the downs.
Feel the emotions,
Without projecting them out.
Emotional maturity.
Conscious living.
Less doing.
More being.
Live in your femininity.
Embrace your creativity.
Leave the insanity.
Find your clarity.
Bring out your ambiguity.
Trust in uncertainty.
Walk away from cruelty.
Be open to opportunity.
Turn to your community.
Make time for serenity.
Ignore the scrutiny.
Surrender to your journey,
Just live.
And learn to let go.
It's okay to find your flow.
Constantly changing.
Be open to it.
The grip of control.
Let it go.
Find your surrender.
Find forgiveness.
Find acceptance.

I will commit to this path,
As I move forward.
Trust and let go.
One step at a time.

His Façade

He used to preach.
Preach how he was a man of God.
He would leave,
Anytime he didn't get what he wants.
He used to preach how he was a man of God.
But anytime he was challenged,
He would put me down.
He used to preach how he was a man of God.
But he loved...
Just loved transactional love.
What's in it for him?
That's how he lives.
He used to preach how he was a man of God.
He would write his songs,
And think he was a God.
He had sayings up on his wall,
Stating that he was a man of integrity.
But he would walk around selfishly,
When he didn't get what he wants.
He would put down other women,
And couldn't see it.
It was all about him.
They were his objects.
He didn't have respect.
Respect for them.
Respect for me.
He then would project,
All of his insecurities.
He would throw his emotions,
All around.

These inappropriate reactions,
Were becoming renowned.
More and more,
Lashing out.
Lashing out at the workers.
Lashing out at me.
Lashing out while out to eat.
Lashing out,
Just because.
So much anger he was throwing around.
He did not want to see himself,
So, he would walk around…
Cheering himself on.
"I am a good guy.
I'm a man of God.
I get served validation,
From other girls I slept with.
I don't care if you don't feel safe…
All that matters is me.
I will make you my punching bag,
And just expect you to take…
Take it like a champ,
Until you leave.
I will still blame you,
And not take any accountability.
I will not say sorry.
And I won't see myself,
Because I take the easy route.
It's easier to use pretty words,
Than to do the internal work.
I will just walk around,
Talking about myself.

Giving myself praise,
As I put you down."
He is a man of God.
This is his façade.

Sticks and Stones

Sticks and stones may break my bones...
But,
Your words you speak...
I will not let them destroy me.
Sticks and stones may break my bones...
But,
Your words you speak...
Go right through me.
Sticks and stones may break my bones...
But,
Your words you speak...
Will not affect me.
Sticks and stones may break my bones...
But,
Your words you speak...
Are making you weak.
Because that kind of energy is extremely heavy.
Those words you speak...
Are weighing you down.
Weighing you down,
More than me.
Because what are you trying to deflect in yourself?
Why are you consuming yourself...
Consuming yourself with my name?
My name coming out of your mouth,
Has more to do with you,
Than it does me.
What does this say?
Say about you?
Sticks and stones may break my bones...

But,
Your words you speak...
Are petty to me.
Sticks and stones may break my bones...
But,
Your words you speak...
Really have nothing to do with me.
How is your character?
Are you a good friend?
Are you a loving person,
Who gives unconditional love?
Can you take your mask off?
I wonder what you look like,
Without your mask?
Under the surface.
Below what you show.
You show to the world.
Everything is for show.
What's on the outside,
Doesn't reflect.
Doesn't reflect who you really are.
Your character.
Your heart,
Is who you really are.
Your heart,
Is it there?
Can you share your heart?
Sticks and stones may break my bones...
But,
Your words you speak...
Don't come from your heart.

Your words you speak...
Are coming from your pain.
And your pain has absolutely nothing to do with me.

The Bed You Made

How does no one see...
This bed you made?
This bed was made...
Made by you.
Created by you.
How does no one see?
That you created this bed.
This bed.
This mess.
You created this.
This is your bed you made.
You made your bed,
Now you must lay.
Lay in it.
Get in and sit.
Lay down in it.
I am done helping to remake this bed.
I am done helping to clean up this mess.
I've done it my whole life.
Put up with it.
Put up with this bed,
That was never mine.
I've gotten out.
I will never return.
I will never help you remake this bed.
Just remember you made this bed.
How no one can see,
That this bed was yours...
How no one can see,
Is beyond me.

How no one can see...
Because the finger is being pointed.
Pointed right at me.
No one wants to see the actual truth.
The truth is that I did not make this bed.
The only thing I did,
Was stop putting up with it.
The only thing I did,
Was walk away.
Walk away from this bed.
Walk away from the mess.

Respond With Silence

How to respond to negative words?
Negative words being spoken about you?
How to respond to this behavior?
The best way...
The very best way...
Silence.
Say nothing,
And live your life beautifully.
Live a beautiful life.
Live a vibrant life.
Live your life,
The life that you want to live.
And you just keep going...
And going...
Not saying a word.
Not feeding into this negativity.
Let them talk.
Let them say whatever they want to say.
All you have to do,
Is nothing.
Respond with silence.
These words they speak,
Have nothing to do with you.
These words they speak,
Is their own pain.
Their pain that they don't want to see.
Silence is the answer.
Respond with silence.
You did everything you could,
To keep it together.

You gave all the love you could,
You poured it all out.
That is what matters,
At the end of the day.
It is now time,
To keep yourself safe.
Stay away from the chaos.
Stay away from the noise.
Stay away from those words being said about you.
Silence is the way.
Use your voice when spoken to.
Defend yourself when you need to.
Confront a situation if is helpful.
But when words are being spoken.
Being spoken about you.
When lies are being spread.
Being spread about you.
When people are talking behind your back,
Let those words roll right off your back.
Turn around and close your eyes.
And just keep living your life.
Let those words roll right off,
As you stay silent.
Stand tall.
Respond with silence.

Who I Used To Be

I am just too tired.
Too tired to care.
I am just tired.
I am tired of surface.
I am tired of putting work in.
If it doesn't flow,
Just let it go.
If it doesn't fit,
Just let go of it.
If it doesn't work,
Just release the grip.
If it doesn't make you happy,
Just walk away.
If it doesn't light you up,
Something else will.
I am just too tired,
Of fixing a situation.
A situation that can't be fixed.
It takes work on both sides.
I am just too tired,
Of sacrificing myself.
I am just too tired,
Of being someone I'm not.
I am just too tired,
Of being brought back.
Back to who I was.
Back to who I used to be.
I am just too tired,
To not be who I am.
This is me now.

I am not who I was.
I am not who I used to be.
I just am not.
Who I used to be,
Was there for everyone else.
Who I used to be,
Put myself aside.
Who I used to be,
Didn't take care of myself.
Who I used to be,
Didn't know who I was.
Who I used to be,
Used to have to work for love.
Who I used to be,
Thought that's how it was.
Who I used to be,
Walked around numb.
Who I used to be,
Didn't feel my emotions.
Who I used to be,
Didn't speak up.
Who I used to be...
Is gone now.

We Are The Parents...

Remember when you attacked me?
And you pretended it didn't happen?
Remember when you called me,
And you told me to get over it?
Remember when you tore me apart,
And then told me to shove it under the rug?
Remember when you did not care one bit,
About how you hurt me?
Remember when you told everyone else,
A completely different story?
Remember when you denied...
Denied my own reality.
Denied actual reality...
Just so you won't feel bad?
Remember when you dismissed me,
Just so you can live your life.
Remember when you wouldn't listen...
Listen to my words?
Remember when I begged you...
Begged you to see your kids?
Remember when you said,
Your house is more important?
More important than spending time with your kids.
Showing your true colors...
Showing your priorities.
Remember when you showed us off...
Showed us off to your friends.
Showed us off like we were objects.
Showed us off like we weren't your kids.
Showed us off to flaunt us.

Flaunt us to make you look good.
Remember when you had everyone fooled...
Except for your kids.
We had it all figured out,
And called it out.
That is when you started your game.
Your game you will play.
You will play it...
Until we all walk away.
You will play it...
While you throw knives.
Knives at your own kids.
Throw these knives.
These knives, that leave wounds.
Wounds you don't care about.
Wounds you don't mend.
Wounds you leave in others,
So that you won't look at yours.
These knives you throw come from your own wounds.
But you will blame everyone else.
Let's create a game.
A game to make us look good.
Because what's on the outside is what matters.
This pretty picture we paint.
We'll paint it for the world.
For all of our friends.
We look like saints,
And we are the victim.
But we are the ones who created this game.
This game our kids don't take part in...
Because they know the truth.
These games that we play in this illusion.

This illusion we live in.
This delusional world,
While we wear our masks.
This façade we put on,
For all of our friends.
This performance we put on,
For everyone to watch.
We pull in our audience,
As we are dishonest.
Because all we care about is this performance.
And how well we play it.
All we care about is who believes us,
As we tear others down.
Our audience doesn't see this,
Because all they see is our performance.
All they see is our pretty little picture.
Our pretty little picture we paint.
All they see is us...
Playing the stars...
The stars that stomp all over their kids.
But only while no one is watching.
We do this in secret,
So that our audience doesn't see.
We do this to hide...
Hide what's really going on.
We tear others down,
If they try to point out reality.
We tear others down,
If they don't read from our script.
If they don't perform perfectly,
And correctly...
They're out.

If they don't agree to play our game.
If they don't agree on our terms.
If they don't agree to wear their mask.
If they don't agree to act.
Act in this play.
Act in this game.
Act in this performance.
We will tear them apart.
We will call them spoiled brats...
We will call them fake and vindictive.
We will think of names to call them,
Because name calling is our favorite.
Our audience doesn't pick up on this...
This name calling and belittlement.
We love to punish and blame,
While no one is watching.
We do this on the sidelines,
And when we're done, we leave with a smile.
This is what makes us feel big.
This is what gives us power to perform in our play.
This is what gives us power,
While our audience cheers us on.
They're cheering us on,
While we wear our masks.
But they have no clue what goes on,
When we take our mask off.
Our audience plays along,
Because this is what they do.
We control our audience.
We control what they see.
We are controlling the narrative...
But our audience doesn't see.

We are the victim.
We are certainly not the villain.
We have done nothing wrong.
We are the parents,
Picking apart our children.
We are the parents,
Name calling our children.
We are the parents,
Who belittles our children.
We are the parents,
Who play mind games with our children.
We are the parents,
Who manipulate our children.
We are the parents,
Who need to feel big.
We are the parents,
Who always save face.
We are the parents,
Who stomp on our children's hearts.
We are the parents,
Who hide all of this.
We are the parents,
Who always show up for our performance.
Our performance is for show,
It is not for love.
(How does no one see?
That this behavior,
Should not be coming from a parent?)
We are the parents who play in this performance...
Please come join us,
And be our audience.

Oh, Those Girls…

Oh,
Those girls…
They don't need love.
They have it figured out,
And they're always there for everyone else.
Oh,
Those girls…
They don't need us.
They can do it all themselves,
And be there for us.
Oh,
Those girls…
We can treat them how we want,
Because they take it…
They always just take it.
Until the day they stop.
Until the day they wake up.
Wake up and realize.
Realize the truth.
They woke up,
And stopped.
Stopped playing our game.
They stopped reading from our script.
They left the cage.
That cage they were in.
That cage we kept them in.
We kept them locked up.
Oh,
Those girls…

Damn them,
They are to blame.
They are this...
And they are that...
All because they left our cage.
They got off that leash.
That leash we had them on.
All tied up...
Tied up to us.
Tied up to perform.
Give them the script.
And send them off.
Off to perform.
Perform for us.
Perform for our audience...
Our family and friends.
Oh,
Those girls...
Damn them again.
There they go,
Standing up for themselves.
This is not what we taught them.
They are not obeying our rules.
Damn those girls...
Off they go,
Spreading their truth.
The truth about us.
The truth we don't want anyone to see.
The truth we don't want anyone to believe.
The truth we've been hiding.
Hiding for years.
Damn those girls.

Running their mouth.
Standing up to us...
Calling everything out.
Oh...
Those girls.
There they go...
Having their own rules.
Having their own life.
Creating their own identity.
This is not what we taught them.
We taught them...
To always, ALWAYS,
Stay in this cage.
Stay where you are put.
Stay on this leash.
We give you this leash,
So that you cannot leave.
Read from this script.
Feed us words...
Pretty words...
That keep us alive.
These pretty words...
Keep us staying big.
Big,
On our pedestal.
Big,
So that you stay small.
We are big.
You are small.
Stay down there...
And follow our rules.
You do not have a voice,

Because you have this script.
This is your role...
Your identity does not go beyond any of this.
Oh,
Those girls.
Can you believe them?
Those spoiled brats...
Walking away.
Walking away from us.
Walking away from all of this?!
This is not what we taught them.
We taught them to stay small.
You listen to us,
As we hold you down.
We hold you down,
With our control.
We rip you to shreds,
As we take your strength.
We take your strength,
So that you can never walk away.
Walking away from us...
Walk away from all of this!!!
How could you!?
Not want to be part of this?
Part of the games...
Part of the chaos...
Part of our drama...
Part of this insanity...
This disfunction...?
How could you leave *this*?!
Oh,
Those girls.

We will find a name to call you,
So that we stay big.
We will find a way,
To keep our power.
We will find a reason to blame you,
So that we stay up on our pedestal.
We will make up lies about you,
So that our show can go on.
Oh,
Those girls...
Effecting our performance.
We will find a way,
To keep our audience.
Oh,
Those girls...
Effecting our roles.
Effecting our games.
These games we play.
But no worries,
We will always make them our scapegoat...
As we stay up high on our pedestal.

"Whatever Makes You Happy"

They had their narrative.
Their narrative of her.
They had their beliefs.
Their beliefs of her.
They would call her names.
Belittle her.
They would put labels on her,
As they put her down.
Creating this narrative.
This narrative of her.
This narrative was about them.
All about them.
This narrative helped them.
Helped them stay big.
Staying big was important.
Important to them.
More important than love.
More important than support.
Instead, they would stay.
Stay up on their pedestal.
They would stay in their pride,
And be filled with envy and shame.
Low vibrations,
They would choose.
Have something to talk about,
Instead of spreading love.
Instead of giving love,
They hand out their putdowns.
Gossip and games,
Became their world.

Condescending and control,
Was what they know.
They know it well.
When approached with the truth,
They would tear her down.
They will stay in their illusion,
No matter what.
They will keep creating this delusion.
This delusional world made them happy.
She will walk away,
As she says…
"Hey…
Whatever makes you happy."

RUN

Oh,
Those games...
These games you play.
I am done,
And I am walking away.
I will not partake in these games you play.
I am done,
And I am walking away.
I don't have the energy,
To play these games.
I don't have the strength,
To figure them out.
I don't have the capacity anymore,
For these games.
I have nothing left inside of me,
To play these games.
These games have to do with you,
And the void inside of you.
You do not have love for yourself,
So how do you love unconditionally?
These games are created,
For the chaos.
The chaos you thrive on.
The chaos you love.
These games are created,
For your entertainment.
Because you are addicted to being vindictive.
You are addicted to chaos and drama.
You are lifted,
When there are problems.

You are addicted to the hormones.
The hormones that are released,
When there is chaos.
The adrenaline you feel,
When you are playing a game...
Is something I recognize now,
And will run from.
I will recognize a game,
As soon as I see it.
I will turn my back,
And I will not play it.
My nervous system,
Shuts right down now...
As soon as I see a game appear.
My nervous system recognizes these games,
From a mile away.
Red flags are waving...
CAUTION. RUN.
I recognize these red flags,
From miles away now.
These games,
Are your fix.
You are addicted to drama.
You are addicted to noise,
And create more problems.
You are completely unaware,
As you act foolishly.
Acting like a child...
Smiling when it is over.
You create these games,
And find people who play them.
Your favorite people are genuine.

Your favorite people are naïve.
Your favorite people are the ones,
Who wear rose-colored glasses.
Your favorite people are the ones,
Who can't see any of it.
Your favorite people are the ones,
Who have trust in you.
Because you are wearing your mask,
As you design this game.
You live in your delusional world,
Up on your pedestal.
High up on your pedestal,
Is where you create these games.
You expect a reaction,
An emotional reaction.
You expect a response,
And not to be called out.
You thrive on the reactions,
In this delusional world you live in.
This delusional world,
Surrounded with red flags.
These red flags signal to me now,
STAY AWAY.
This is when I turn my back,
And walk away.

She Painted This Picture

She painted this picture,
Of who she wanted to become.
She painted this picture,
And this is who she became.
She painted this picture.
This beautiful picture.
This beautiful visual,
Of who she wanted to be.
Who she wanted to become.
Who she wanted to run to.
Attached to nothing,
Leaving codependency.
A clear horizon.
A sky full of color.
Every color of the sunset.
The sunset...
A constant.
She could rely on this.
The end of a day.
The sunrise.
This constant.
The beginning of a new day.
These beautiful constants,
With anything in between.
Anything can happen,
She is open to it.
This beautiful place,
She envisioned for herself.
Herself,
She needed to grieve.

To become her true self.
She painted this picture.
This beautiful picture,
Of where she wanted to go.
Leaving the noise,
And finding solitude.
Removing her walls,
Opening her heart.
This is who she is.
Who she is at her core.
Connecting with nature.
So spiritual.
Becoming soft...
Leaving the strong girl,
To soften into this girl.
Getting to know nurture,
As she forgets how to run.
Learning to stay,
As she no longer knows how to go.
GO.
GO.
GO.
Always on the go,
Autopilot on.
Understanding and compassion.
Acceptance and love.
Leaving those low vibrations,
As she lifts herself up.
Higher and higher,
Into her picture.
Her picture she painted.
Painted for herself.

Leaving it all behind,
Embracing this clarity.
Loving her solitude.
Loving herself.
Holding her worth,
In the palm of her hand.
Holding her empowerment,
As she leaves her old world.

Your Soul

You can't fight.
Fight it off.
You can't tune it out.
You can't control it.
Your soul is your soul.
It is always there.
It knows what is best.
What is best for you.
You can't shut it off.
You can't run from it.
It will scream and scream,
Until you listen.
It will stop you dead in your tracks,
If you are trying to push it away.
It will shut your body down,
If you keep repeating patterns.
It will shut everything off,
Until you sit in silence.
Sit in silence,
And hear it all.
Your soul knows.
It has always known.
It has always spoken.
It just wasn't as loud.
It wasn't as loud,
Because of the noise.
It wasn't as loud,
Because of the chaos.
It wasn't as loud,
Because it was covered in pain.

The more you healed,
The louder it became.
The more layers you peeled away,
The clearer it became.
Your soul,
It will rise.
Rise inside of you.
Your soul,
It knows...
What is best for you.
Your soul.
Your calling.
This is you.

Her Story Of Her Life

She must own her story.
She must own it all.
She must be confident in her story,
And stand tall.
This is what came.
Came to her.
This is what God brought.
Brought to her.
She must own her story,
What happened in her life.
She must understand,
Nothing happened TO her...
But FOR her.
She must understand,
And have compassion.
Compassion for herself,
Through it all.
This compassion came at the end...
At the end of looking at her pain.
This compassion filled her heart.
Filled her heart,
For herself.
She finally found compassion.
She found acceptance and love.
As she puts it all behind her,
So that she can move on.
She must own her story,
For her to move on.
She must own it,
And love it.

She must own her story,
For her to find empowerment.
She found her empowerment,
Inside of herself.
Everything came,
From within.
Everything came,
From seeing it all.
Everything came,
Inside of stillness.
Inside of solitude.
She needed silence.
She will hold her heart,
As she stands by…
Stands by her story.
Her story of her life.

Let it Roll In

When you let go of everything.
Everyone you know.
Letting go becomes easy.
Easy to do.
Let it all go.
Not holding on...
Just letting it be.
Be what it is.
Let everyone just be.
Be who they are.
Let everyone live,
The way they want to live.
Let everything roll.
Roll off your back.
It is not your problem.
It is not yours to take on.
Let them act the way they want to act...
You can choose what is best for you.
Not everything is meant...
Meant to stay.
Not everything is here to be permanent.
It is all temporary...
It is all just a flow.
Just let it roll in...
Let it roll out.
Worry about you...
Let everything else go.
The things that hurt.
Let them go.
The things that don't work.

Let them go too.
The things that cause stress…
Not for you.
The things that make you feel good…
Move towards that.
The things that light you up…
Those are your things.
Hold onto faith,
As you spread your wings.
You are free.
Free to fly.
Spread your wings,
As you let everything go.
Find what is yours,
As you fly free.

Blooming Through It All

Why don't you like me?
Because I spoke my truth.
Why don't you like me?
Because I've stopped accepting abuse.
Why don't you like me?
Because I am stepping away.
Why don't you like me?
Because I'm standing up for myself.
Why don't you like me?
Because I am living my life.
Why don't you like me?
Because I see who you are.
Why don't you like me?
Because I've stopped sacrificing myself.
Why don't you like me?
Because I spoke words you don't want to hear.
Why don't you like me?
Because I challenge you.
Challenge society.
Challenge this family.
Because I walked away from black or white.
Because I live with shades of grey.
Because I found beautiful colors.
Beautiful colors that stand out around me.
Because I became this wildflower?
This wildflower you can't predict.
This wildflower you can't control.
This wildflower who stands tall.
Stands tall in the storms.
This wildflower who doesn't die,

Without your water.
Who doesn't die without your attention.
Who doesn't die without your love.
This wildflower, who grows.
Grows through it all.
Grows through too much water...
And not enough.
Grows through hurricanes,
And times of stillness.
This wildflower remains.
Remains on her own.
This wildflower keeps blooming.
Blooming through it all.
Bloom after bloom,
After she falls.
This wildflower perks up,
After the noise.
After the chaos.
This wildflower keeps her beauty,
After she should have fallen.
Fallen and wilted,
And lost her color.
This wildflower who should still be...
Still be beautiful.
Still be strong.
Still be standing.
Standing tall.
This wildflower is...
She just is...
More beautiful than ever,
Ever before.
Without your water polluting her.

Without your water killing her.
Without your attention,
Breaking her.
Without your winds,
Blowing her down.
This wildflower does better without any of that.
On her own,
This wildflower stands.
Creating her own environment.
Getting her own water.
Fulfilling herself with her own nutrients.
Now that she's stopped accepting pollution.
Now that she's stopped sipping your water.
Now that she's this beautiful wildflower.
This wildflower,
She became.
This wildflower,
She is.
This wildflower,
She'll stay...
Stay without the pollution.

This Road To Nowhere

Driving her car.
Windows down.
The beach on her right.
Lines of palm trees on her left.
This empty road.
This road ahead of her.
Her hair, blowing in the wind.
She is free.
This road leads to nowhere.
She has no final destination.
Who knows where she'll end up.
Wherever she ends up is where she will be.
This road to nowhere.
No destination.
Just stops along the way.
A stop here.
A stop there.
This horizon out ahead of her.
This horizon is clear.
This horizon she sees.
This road to nowhere.
This long winding road.
The water on her right.
The trees on her left.
Leaving the city,
Because she didn't belong.
She didn't belong there.
The chaos and the noise,
Drove her away.
Drove her to leave.

Leave this insanity.
This insanity that she knew.
She will leave it behind.
She knew she needed to leave.
She knew she couldn't stay.
She knew her place was far away.
Far away from here.
Far from the noise.
Far from the chaos.
Far from this place.
This place she knew.
Driving away,
Not looking back.
Driving away,
With her windows down.
Driving away,
Without a care in the world.
Driving away.
Away from that world.
This world that she knew.
This world was not hers.
This world she did not belong in.
This world of noise.
This world of chaos.
Driving away.
Away from this place.
Driving away.
Along this road.
This road with no destination.
This road with no expectations.
This road is unknown.
This road is not paved.

This road she is on.
She is driving away.
Away from this world.
Driving to God knows where.
Driving to wherever she ends up.
Wherever she ends up,
On this road.
This road to nowhere.
This road of the unknown.
This road to freedom.
This freedom she found.

She Couldn't Grow There

She couldn't grow there.
There,
Where she was.
She couldn't grow where she knew.
The only place she knew.
She couldn't be who she needed to become.
Not where she was.
She couldn't grow there,
With all the expectations.
She couldn't bloom there.
There,
In that cage.
She needed to leave.
She needed out.
She needed to fly.
She needed to roam free.
She needed freedom.
Her soul needed space.
Her soul needed nature.
Her soul needed the sun.
Her soul needed grounding.
Her soul needed silence.
Her soul needed solitude.
Her soul needed a quiet place.
This quiet place to rest.
This quiet place to be.
This quiet place to bloom.
This quiet place to reflect.
This quiet place to love.
Love herself and the world.

Find compassion and learn to forgive.
Become authentic and true.
True to herself.
True to the world.
Let go of who she was.
Peeling back the layers.
The layers to her soul.
Listening to her intuition.
It became louder.
It started as a whisper.
Now,
This voice...
So clear.
Her intuition guides her.
Every minute of the day.
This voice.
Her voice.
Leads the way.

This Is Her Way

This is her way.
Her way of feeling seen.
This is her way.
Her way of feeling heard.
This is her way,
Of sharing herself.
Her truth.
Her voice.
Her vulnerability.
This is her way of acknowledging her wounds.
This is her way,
Of loving herself.
Loving herself in ways she has never loved before.
This is her way,
Of spreading love to the world.
Love and healing she gives away.
Vibrance and serenity,
She will carry with her.
Acceptance and forgiveness,
Has come upon her.
This is her way of seeing this illusion.
This illusion she lived in,
Her whole life.
Moving away from black and white,
Finding her favorite shade of grey.
This is her way,
Of putting her mask down.
This is her.
All parts of her.
Finding her wholeness,

Inside of stillness.
Discovering herself.
Discovering her heart.
Her heart without walls,
Feeling it all.
Unconditional love,
As she falls.
Living without armor.
Feeling safe.
Safe inside of herself,
As she finds trust.
Her very own trust,
That she's never felt before.
Finding her trust as she surrenders it all.
Surrenders to herself,
As she believes in herself.
Holding her faith.
Taking a breath.
Breathe in.
Breathe out.
This is it.
Light.
Her light.
She is free.

Thank you.
Sending you empowerment.

I dedicate this book to all the "cycle breakers."
Making new choices is extremely hard, brave, & courageous.
You all are beautiful.
Keep being you.